KEVIN'S LAST WALK

A FATHER'S FINAL JOURNEY WITH HIS SON

IT'S ALL GOOD!

Barry Adkins

Printed in the United States of America
Printed by Snowfall Press
Published by KLW Publishing, LLC
Book cover and design by Zanne Kennedy
Book design by Chris O'Byrne

ISBN 9781936539055

www.kevinslastwalk.com

When my son, Kevin, died I had two choices: I could curl up in the corner, become a "victim," and let others tend to me or I could do my best to make something very good come from his death. I chose the latter.

This book is dedicated to Kevin, whose death has taught me that life holds no guarantees, and that ordinary people can do extraordinary things when called upon to do so.

Acknowledgments

The author would like to acknowledge all those who helped turn this old redneck's ramblings into something readable.

My friend, Steve McMoyler, who was the first to say, "No, dude, this isn't good enough."

Lucy Dale, who preached patience and reminded me over and over that writing a book takes time.

Our neighbor and friend, Loreen Coons, who should be teaching writing somewhere.

My editor, Chris O'Byrne, who probably wishes he had looked my manuscript over a little more closely before he gave me a quote.

John Mickler, who is a good enough friend to say, "You're going to write this book or else."

I guess there is one more person I should probably acknowledge and that is my blushing bride, Bev. She will tell you that I am living proof that next to every good man is a better woman. By the way, she also had a great deal of input on this acknowledgement.

Table of Contents

Chapter 1

Introduction

My son Kevin was like most teenagers. He never believed that anything could happen to him. He thought he was ten foot tall and bulletproof.

I often gave him a speech about safety, being careful, and of course, clean underwear. His standard answer was, "Yeah, yeah, Dad, I know; you don't have to tell me again. I know what I am doing."

But Kevin was wrong, so horribly wrong; he didn't know what he was doing. It would cost him his life and alter my perfect little life in a way I never would have imagined.

This is our story.

KEVIN'S LAST WALK

Chapter 2

A Letter to Kevin

Dear Kevin,

Well son, it was one incredible journey. I kept you close to me all the way. Your ashes were there in my backpack to give me strength and courage every time I spoke. We walked together through barren deserts, withering wind, snow and rain storms, up over high mountain passes, and down through beautiful sun-drenched mountain valleys for the final time.

I played back so many fond memories of you as I walked. Memories of the day you were born, your many baseball and soccer games, trips to the county fair with your pigs, sitting at our dinner table talking about life, our many hunting trips together, hugging you so tight after you graduated from high school, and yes, the last time I saw you alive. I hugged you and told you I loved you and to be careful. I then stood on our front porch and watched as you drove away for the final time.

At the viewing before the memorial I was there, but I didn't go in. I stood outside with friends and family—hugging, laughing, and crying. I chose to not see you lying in a casket, but to remember you as you lived: your love for a good laugh, a good friend, and for life.

You taught me many things in life about being a father and what it means to love a child. Your death has taught me how deep that love goes and that life holds no guarantees. You taught me that God has a plan for each of us and sometimes someone must die so that others might live. You are no longer with us physically, but you will always be in our hearts.

Love,
The Dad

Chapter 3

That Fateful Night

Kevin started the process of moving out on his own on a July day when the sun seemed to cover half the sky. He spent most of the day like many teenagers in the Phoenix area: at the Salt River with friends.

The Salt River flows through central Arizona and the Phoenix area. The river is dammed in several places, so the water flow is, well, perfect for a lazy summer afternoon in some inner tubes.

A month earlier, Kevin had met my financial requirements, so I agreed to cosign a loan on a new truck. When he found his truck at a local dealership, he called to tell me all about it. "Dad, you have to come see it; it's a red Ford Ranger and it's awesome!"

Buying from a dealership meant that I would have to go down and help him negotiate the final price and sign the papers—not exactly one of my favorite things to do. Once we agreed on the price, we sat down in a cramped office with the finance guy to sign the papers. The finance guy looked at me and asked if I needed any life insurance. I was rather annoyed with his question and told him that I didn't need any life insurance. My wife will do just fine if something happens to me. He looked at me and said, "I'm not talking about you; I'm talking about your son." I rather indignantly told him we didn't need life insurance on Kevin; 18-year-old boys don't die.

I was so very wrong. They do die. Kevin would not live long enough to make a single payment on his new truck.

When Kevin got home from the river, he took a

shower and started packing a few belongings in his new truck. Those belongings included his bed, TV, and a piece of junk dresser he'd just bought at a thrift store.

For some reason, he thought that he needed to leave his dresser with us. His dresser definitely looked like it belonged to a guy. When we got it, Kevin didn't like it very much. He said it "looked like a girl's dresser" because it was white. He wanted to make it look more like a guy's dresser, so he and I decided to make it look rustic. To do this, we took it out to the garage and proceeded to take a hammer, a grinder, and whatever else we could find to this dresser. We gave it a rustic look all right. Kevin took great pleasure in this exercise.

Kevin's friend, Craig, and I finished helping him pack the first load. When Kevin was done, he came back inside, went into his room and picked up a clean pair of jeans off of the floor and threw them in the dryer to de-wrinkle. I realize that most teenagers always pick their dirty clothes up and put them in the hamper, but not Kevin. Kevin had to walk by the hamper to leave his room, but the dirty clothes still didn't make it in the hamper. I also realize that most teenagers always fold their clothes and put them away as soon as they come out of the dryer, but Kevin was different. Kevin had two piles of clothes on the floor in his room: one pile was his dirty clothes and the other was the aforementioned "clean, wrinkled clothes."

While his jeans were de-wrinkling, he came in and told me he was going to brush his teeth now because he didn't want to take his toothbrush with him. He said, "I'll be back tomorrow and get it." I have never forgotten those words and I think about them often. Why didn't he want to take his toothbrush with him? I have often wondered about this. Maybe it was his way of putting my mind at ease as my youngest child (okay, my baby) moved out. He put on his jeans, gave me a hug, and said, "I love you, Dad." I told him I loved him, too, and to be careful. I walked out front with him, stood on the front porch, and watched him drive away.

It was the last time I saw him alive.

As one would expect, I think about those final moments that I saw him alive. Maybe there was something else I could have said or done that could have changed it all, something that would have caused Kevin to do something different that night—anything. I think about how I don't remember much about the sunset that night—the last sunset he would ever see—and that he would not live to see another sunrise.

I guess we should all appreciate beautiful sunsets and sunrises because we never know when it will be the last one we ever see with the ones we love.

I no longer look at dates the same. When I look at a date on a piece of paper or someone talks about things that have happened in the past, my first thought is, *Was Kevin alive then?*

That night the guys he moved in with decided to have a housewarming party for Kevin. They had a keg of beer and some Southern Comfort. There were somewhere between 15 and 25 kids at this party along with a few adults. The ages ranged from 15 to 28. Some time around midnight, they decided to do some shots. Kevin did several double shots of the Southern Comfort.

A short time later, he passed out. The kids at the party laid him in his bed, on his side, in case he vomited. They then decided to play a joke on him, so they went in to his room and shaved his head and his legs.

Kevin's friend, Craig, was worried about him, so he

went in to check on him a few times. When he checked on him around 4:00 a.m, he found him blue and not breathing. The first 911 call indicated difficulty breathing. By the next call, he was not breathing. My son was pronounced dead on arrival at the hospital while I slept peacefully in my bed.

Chapter 4

Sunday Mornings Will Never Be the Same

The next morning, my wife Beverly and I were sitting in our living room doing what many couples do on Sunday morning: drinking coffee, reading the newspaper with our feet up, and planning our day. Although I don't recall specifically, I would guess our planned day included a trip to church and the hardware store on the way home, maybe a little yard work, and if all went really well, a nap. I was sitting in our blue, leather recliner that has a nice view of our backyard, the same recliner I was sitting in when Kevin and I talked about him moving out.

A few weeks earlier, Kevin had walked into the living room and sat down in our brown chair next to the large picture window with a panoramic view of our backyard. He said, "I can't believe I graduated from high school and I'm finally starting my life." He then told me he wanted to move out. He was going to move into a rented house with three other guys. He had looked at his budget and could easily afford it. I told him I didn't think it was a good idea, but for selfish reasons. I guess he was like many 18-year-old guys, and felt like it was time to get out from under dad's thumb and start living. He often went to visit his sisters at their apartments and would come home and tell me about how cool it was that they were living on their own. I shouldn't have been surprised, but I was.

This was very different from when I left home. A few months after I graduated from high school, my parents decided to move to Homer, Alaska and I went along with them. When we arrived in Homer, my parents rented a small three-bedroom mobile home (call it what it was: a

9

trailer house). The boys' bedroom had barely enough room for two beds and there were three of us, with me being the oldest. Hmm, maybe it was time for me to leave.

As I sat in my easy chair with my feet up enjoying the view of our backyard, the doorbell rang. Bev and I gave each other a puzzled look. Who could that be? We weren't expecting any company.

It was the Gilbert Police. There were two police officers and someone dressed in civilian clothes. I joked with them and invited them to come in, but they didn't laugh. I figured this had to be about one of the neighbors or a dog barking. It had to be something along those lines. There could be no other reason for the Gilbert Police to be at my house at 8:30 on a Sunday morning, could there?

One of the officers walked cautiously into our living room and stood in front of the same brown chair Kevin had sat in when he told me he wanted to move out, while the other two sort of stood back in the entryway of our house. The officer stared at Bev, who was still sitting down. I sat down to hear what the officer had to say. The officer was clearly nervous and spoke very softly and slowly. He said he had some bad news as he continued to stare at Bev. He said, "There has been an accident and your son is dead." For a moment, I thought he was talking about one of her sons from a previous marriage. She asked who and his answer took my breath away. It was my son Kevin.

At that moment, it seemed like my heart had been ripped from my chest. My arms and legs seemed to disappear as the blood drained from them. It was as if the camera was zooming out and the world suddenly felt as if I wasn't in it any more, like I was watching from a place very distant. As I write this, I am sitting in the same recliner and it feels like he just told me.

The officer handed Kevin's driver's license to Bev who looked at it and handed it to me. There's something pretty final when an officer hands you your child's driver's license, because until that moment, you are hoping and praying that this is all a big mistake; they must have the wrong house, maybe they should be two streets over, or maybe they're in the wrong town, you need to find Kevin Atkins, not my Kevin Adkins. The young man that died is not my Kevin Adkins; it's a Kevin Adkins that lives anywhere but here. But when they hand you your son's driver's license, you know there is no mistake—your son is gone and you will never see him again.

It felt to me like time was standing still, like this couldn't be happening. I kept thinking, *This can't be happening, this just simply can't be happening.* I needed Kevin to be there, to not be gone. I needed to give him another hug and tell him again that I loved him so very, very much. If he was going to die, I needed time to prepare. Time. That thing that I wanted so desperately to rewind so I could go back to when he was alive. I didn't need to go way back in time, just to the night before when he was alive and my little world was good. I had it so good and I needed to go back to that night and make things good again. It was my job as his father to protect him and to help him live a long and happy life. I needed to do that. Maybe I could back up time and God could take me instead of him. Kevin didn't deserve to die so young. I had lived a good life. In fact, I remember thinking a few weeks before Kevin had died that I had lived a good life. I had experienced the wildernesses of Alaska and Montana, traveled to Asia, Europe, and the Middle East. I had enjoyed the experience of parenthood, the pain of divorce, and found the love of my life. I guess most folks would say I had lived the American dream.

11

God could take me instead.

If God were a good God, He would take me instead. It seemed much fairer to me, but sadly, people who don't deserve to die still die, and life is not always fair.

I had always been there for Kevin. I'd been there when he lost his first tooth and took his first steps. I was there to cheer him up when things didn't go his way and I was there to discipline him when he needed it, to encourage him when school didn't go well. I was also there to teach him how to throw a football, swing a bat, and shoot a gun.

How could I not be there to protect him from this? How could I let him die? How could I not be there to say one last goodbye? I had said a casual, "Bye," and told Kevin that I loved him the night before, but I didn't say goodbye.

One of us finally found the strength to ask the officer what had happened. The officer told us that the probable cause of death was alcohol poisoning. We found out later that Kevin's blood alcohol level was .36%, which is very drunk, but the coroner told me that they have seen as low as .25% kill teenagers here in the Phoenix area.

A couple of years later, I was out walking and ran into this officer. We talked at length about that morning. It was the first time he had ever had to do something like that. He told me how he doesn't normally go home and talk about his day, but on this day he did tell his wife about what happened. He said that as a police officer you come to realize that alcohol can change lives in an instant. One minute someone is headed home from work or on their way to the store, and in an instant, they're gone. In our case, we were sitting in our living room enjoying Sunday morning and in an instant, Kevin was gone.

How was I going to find the strength to go on or the words to share the news of his death?

Chapter 5

Things No Parent Should Ever Have to Do

Now came the excruciating process of spreading the news that my son was dead. I called my ex-wife's mother and told her what had happened. My ex-wife and I were not exactly close, and I felt it better for her family to tell her. This left me to share the tragic news with his sisters, Sarah and Cassandra.

You knew that my children all loved each other by the way they argued. They would be at the dinner table arguing and then one of them would say, "Hey, let's go to the movies." And then off they would go to the movies together.

Kevin was the designated bug and critter killer for his sisters. Cassandra came home late one night and found a cockroach in the bathroom. She went in and woke Kevin up and talked him into killing it for her.

Sarah once called me at work to report she had seen a small snake in her room. I wasn't going to be home for a while so Kevin was dispatched to take care of the problem. Kevin did get the snake out of her room, but we never did figure out how it got in there in the first place.

Kevin also enjoyed scaring his sisters, especially Sarah. When Sarah was 16 and Kevin was 14, she got a job at the local McDonalds. At the time, the only vehicle she was allowed to drive was my 1981 Ford pickup. It had a manual transmission and locks on the doors that were just decoration by that point. She called me one night while she was at work. She was in a panic because she had gone out to get in the truck and it had been moved. I assured her that everything was okay. When I hung up the phone, I

13

immediately called Kevin, who was staying with his friend, Blake, that night. I asked Kevin if he knew anything about the truck being moved. Kevin started laughing. The mystery had been solved.

The "Urban Assault Vehicle" that they all had to learn to drive.

Kevin shared his birthday with Sarah. They were both born in February, two years apart. Because Sarah and Kevin were both born on the same day, we always celebrated their birthdays together. I suspect they didn't always like this. Each year one would pick the birthday cake they wanted, and the other would pick the meal. As you might imagine, birthdays for Sarah and for us are quite different now.

Kevin and Sarah's last birthday celebration together.

I knew that telling his sisters would be difficult and it turned out to be, by far, the most difficult thing I had to do.

I was in no condition to drive and this wasn't the sort of news one passes along over the phone. I needed to get to Cassandra's apartment. She wouldn't be surprised to see me as I had planned to stop by that morning anyway. Sarah was at work and I couldn't get in contact with her, so I called her boyfriend, Ed, and told him to go get her and meet me at Cassandra's apartment. I didn't feel that it would be right to tell her at work.

I walked into Kevin's room and stood there looking at the things he had left behind: golf clubs, cowboy hats, baseball hats, clothes in the closet and on the floor, notes on his wall, and the gun cabinet he made in high school (with a lot of help from his teacher). It's difficult to explain, but the room still smelled like Kevin. I took a deep breath and tried to focus on the task at hand.

One of Kevin's best friends was Blake. I called Blake's dad, Kelly, and asked him to come over to the house as soon as possible. I didn't tell him what it was about, but I guess he knew it was bad by the tone of my voice. When Kelly arrived, I told him the news. He immediately got on the phone to his wife, Brenda, and told her Kevin had died. Blake was out of town at the time, fishing with a friend in Michigan. Before Kelly could contact him, he heard about Kevin through the friend he was fishing with. When I was a boy, communication was quite different. I remember hearing about the death of a classmate several days after he died in a car accident. Today, it seems almost every student has a cell phone, so word of Kevin's death spread quickly.

When Kevin was in high school, one of his friends was killed in a car accident. Word of his death spread quickly. It seemed hundreds of students gathered at the accident scene within minutes.

As we drove to Cassandra's apartment, I leaned against the door of Kelly's truck, stared out the window, and didn't say much. What could I say?

My son was dead.

I stared out at the mountains and thought about what I had just heard. How was I going to tell his sisters and how were they going to handle this? I kept thinking, *This just can't be happening. This has to be a bad dream. Maybe I've been in a car accident and I'm dreaming all of this.* I needed time to stand still so that I could gather my thoughts. I needed to figure out how to get out of this nightmare. *I can do it, I know I can,* I thought. *This stuff happens to other people, but it doesn't happen to me.*

When we got to Cassandra's, she was surprised to see Bev and my friend, Kelly, with me.

Cassandra gave birth to my grandson, a handsome baby boy by the name of Collin, in October of Kevin's senior year in high school. When Collin was born, Cassandra was working and going to medical assistant's school. This meant that we had to watch Collin at night while she was at school. My wife Bev and I would take care of him until 8:30 or 9:00 p.m. and then Kevin would take over. Many nights when Cassandra got home, Kevin would be asleep in her room with Collin. Kevin would then have to get up in the morning and go to school himself. Sadly, Collin will have no memory of his uncle Kevin.

As we walked into Cassandra's apartment, Bev immediately picked Collin up out of his high chair and took him in the bedroom. I started crying before I could tell Cassandra and she started crying. I put my hands on her shoulders and told her that Kevin was in heaven. She slid down the wall until she was sitting on the floor, sobbing with her hands on her face.

A short time later, Sarah arrived with her boyfriend Ed. She knew it was bad news when she walked in. I told her that Kevin was in heaven. She fell to the floor and started crying and asking someone to wake her up. "Somebody please, please wake me up," she cried. She was hoping it was all a bad dream, that bad dream that we all have had and we wake up and think, *Wow, I'm glad that was just a dream.* Sadly, for Sarah and for us, it wasn't a bad dream. Her brother was gone and he wasn't coming back.

Cassandra then told us that Kevin had left a voicemail

for her the night before. In that voicemail he talked about how drunk he was and about how much he loved his nephew Collin—who was nine months old when he died—and how he "loved that kid more than anything in the world." You could hear people laughing and talking in the background. If you listened to the voicemail, you would think, *Aw, no big deal, just a bunch of kids having a party and getting drunk.* No big deal, except somebody died that night, and that somebody was my son Kevin.

We made our way back home. To make matters worse, the power went out at our house that day. I don't recall how long it was off, but it was off long enough that we decided to go over to Kelly's house until the power came back on.

I decided that I needed to go to the house where Kevin died and retrieve his new truck. When I arrived at the house, there were still police officers and a few people around. I had a key to his truck so I didn't need to go into the house—the house where Kevin had spent his last night, taken his last breath, and gone to be with God.

I never went into the house where he died. I asked some of his friends to bring his belongings back, everything except the bed. I didn't want to see the bed where Kevin had taken his last breath, the bed he laid dying in while the party was still going on.

As I drove his truck home, I thought about how I never test drove it when we went to buy it. Kevin asked me to take it for a test drive, but I told him that if it was the truck he wanted, I probably wouldn't be able to talk him out of it anyway.

Part of me died that Sunday morning and life has not been the same since. How can life go on? I woke up the next day amazed that the sun came up, that the TV still

18

worked, that people were driving down the road by my house as if it were a normal Monday. Kevin had just spent his first night in heaven. I wondered what it was like. I was his father and had done my best to protect him, to teach him, and to take care of him. He was now someplace where I couldn't protect him, to advise him on what to do, to hear him, to… just touch him. The Bible teaches us to let go and let God. Easy to say, not so easy to do when your son has just gone to be with God.

I can only describe the next few days as very dark. I wanted so much to be with Kevin, but I couldn't, not until God called me. I no longer feared dying. There was very little eating or sleeping. The phone rang constantly and there were people coming in and out all the time, but it was all a blur to me. I needed time alone: time to think, time to breathe, time to maybe wake myself up from this nightmare. I couldn't think straight or focus. Nothing seemed right. Life was still going on, but none of it made any sense. Nothing felt the same. Nothing could be the same for me.

I needed my son so desperately.

Chapter 6

"Something Very Good Will Come From This"

I was sleeping soundly a little before 4:00 a.m. two days after my son had died. I was awakened by what I thought was a chill. I pulled the covers up and tried to go back to sleep. I then felt chills over my entire body as I rolled over and found myself somewhat frozen in place. It was then that I felt a presence, like someone was in the room staring at me. I knew it was Kevin. I can't tell you how I knew it was him because I never heard him speak, nor did I see his face. I was now completely awake and I guess I sort of felt his thoughts. I know that this sounds very "un-Hollywood" but it's the only way I know to describe it. I suppose it makes sense (if one can make sense of these things), since Kevin's spirit was no longer in his physical body.

There was a sensation of a bright light, but I didn't see the light. This presence, that was Kevin, wanted me to know he didn't suffer. He seemed to be very excited, happy, and at peace. It was then that Kevin made it clear that something very good was going to come from this. I was left with the impression that Kevin knew what "something very good" was and that I would be very pleased. Kevin also seemed very pleased that he knew and I didn't! I told him that I loved him and missed him. Then in an instant, before I could say goodbye, he was gone. Afterwards, I had a very intense headache, but felt much more at peace. I didn't feel any fear during this incident, only a profound understanding that we will indeed meet again on the other side.

I believe that this occurred at the exact time of his

death, two days later (somewhere around 4:00 a.m. is when he was first found) so that I would know it was him.

This is where the "something very good" I spoke of at Kevin's memorial came from. This incident is what turned things around for me. I can't say that this made everything okay, because it didn't, but it did help a great deal, and for lack of a better term, gave me a mission. Knowing that "something very good" would come from this is what has kept me going. It's also important to understand that "something very good" did not come from me, it came from Kevin. I would love to take credit for it, but I can't and I won't. I am only passing it along. At the time of this event, I was mired in a state of self pity and absolute shock. It's also important to understand that "something very good" may have nothing to do with alcohol abuse, Kevin, or our family.

Every time I speak publicly, I talk about something very good. When you do your "something very good" for Kevin, it needs to come from the heart and be yours and yours alone. I do not want to limit anyone's thinking. As I said at the memorial, "That is what you can do for us and for Kevin."

Why God granted me this one favor, I will never know. My best guess is that He knew that I was going to need some help and as the saying goes, He "brought the Cavalry." Without a doubt, it was a life changing experience for me.

Something Very Good

Something very good will come from this
Part of me died that morning when I got the news
His job here on earth was through
None of us here knew what to do
He touched so many lives
He had no idea
Made so many people smile
Still, he left for higher places
We will remember his smiling face
He is there in pictures and in paper
He is there in video and in words
He is in our hearts and in our dreams
We see him in the trees
We see him in the stars
He floats by us on a cloud
We feel him in the wind
He will always be there
I never heard him say it,
But something very good will come from this
He was there; I know it and I felt it
He was there in the room
When my heart was filled with gloom
And now that part that died is growing back
Something very good will come from this

You never know when a random act of kindness can turn a life around. The following story has floated around on the Internet for some time. I am not sure about the origin of this story or whether it's a true story, but it does help to drive home my point about doing "something very good" for Kevin. I printed this out and gave it to Kevin several years earlier. It was among the things hanging on the wall in his room when he passed away.

One day, when I was a freshman in high school, I saw a kid from my class was walking home from school. His name was Kyle. It looked like he was carrying all of his books. I thought to myself, Why would anyone bring home all his books on a Friday? He must really be a nerd. I had quite a weekend planned (parties and a football game with my friend the next afternoon), so I shrugged my shoulders and went on.

As I was walking, I saw a bunch of kids running toward him. They ran at him, knocking all his books out of his arms, and tripping him so he landed in the dirt. His glasses went flying, and I saw them land in the grass about ten feet from him. He looked up and I saw this terrible sadness in his eyes. My heart went out to him. I jogged over to him as he crawled around looking for his glasses, and I saw a tear in his eye.

As I handed him his glasses, I said, "Those guys are jerks. They really should get lives." He looked at me and said, "Hey, thanks." There was a big smile on his face. It was one of those smiles that showed real gratitude. I helped him pick up his books, and asked him where he lived. As it turned out, he lived near me, so I asked him why I had never seen him before. He said he had gone to private school before now. I would have never hung out with a private school kid before. We talked all the way home, and I carried his books. He turned out to be a pretty cool kid. I asked him if he wanted to play football on Saturday with my friends and me. He said yes. We hung out all weekend and the more I got to know Kyle, the more I liked him. And my friends thought the same of him.

Monday morning came, and there was Kyle with the huge stack of books again. I stopped him and said, "Dang boy, you are gonna really build some serious muscles with this pile of books everyday!" He just laughed and handed me half the books. Over the next four years, Kyle and I became best friends. When we were seniors, we began to think about college. Kyle decided on Georgetown, and I was going to Duke. I knew that we would always be friends, that the miles would never be a problem. He was going to be a doctor, and I was going for business on a football scholarship. Kyle was Valedictorian of our class. I teased him all the time about being a nerd. He had to prepare a speech for graduation. I was so glad it wasn't me having to get up there and speak.

On graduation day, I saw Kyle. He looked great. He was one of those guys that really found himself during high school. He filled out and actually looked good in glasses. He had more dates than me and all the girls loved him. Boy, sometimes I was jealous. Today was one of those days. I could see that he was nervous about his speech, so I smacked him on the back and said, "Hey, big guy, you'll be great!" He looked at me with one of those looks (the really grateful ones) and smiled. "Thanks," he said.

As he started his speech, he cleared his throat, and began. "Graduation is a time to thank those who helped you make it through those tough years—your parents, your teachers, your siblings, maybe a coach—but mostly your friends. I am here to tell all of you that being a friend to someone is the best gift you can give them. I'm going to tell you a story."

I just looked at my friend with disbelief as he told the story of the first day we met. He had planned to kill himself over the weekend. He talked of how he had cleaned out his locker so his Mom wouldn't have to do it later and was carrying his stuff home. He looked hard at me and gave me a little smile. "Thankfully, I was saved. My friend saved me from doing the unspeakable."

I heard the gasp go through the crowd as this handsome, popular boy told us all about his weakest moment. I saw his mom and dad looking at me and smiling that same grateful smile. Not until that moment did I realize its depth. Never underestimate the power of your actions. With one small gesture you can change a person's life.

I encourage everyone that reads this book to find their "something very good" and do it. I would prefer that you use your imagination, but let me also give you a few ideas of little things you can do to brighten up someone's day.

Today and every day from now on, when you get home or when you leave, give your loved ones a hug and tell them you love them. As I now know all too well, there are no guarantees that they will always be there. This is easy enough, isn't it?

Next time your grandparents or parents have a birthday, or for Christmas, make them something: write them a poem, draw, sing, etc. Spend time with them. I promise they'll love it and you'll be doing something very good.

The Father's Day just before Kevin passed away, the kids wrote down their favorite memories of me on a piece of paper and put them in a jar. We sat and read them together on Father's Day. You could do the same for your family or friends.

Chapter 7

Kevin's Memorial

Visiting a funeral home to discuss your child's funeral is something I wouldn't wish on anyone. How does one make a rational decision the day after their child has died? After considerable discussion, we decided to have an open casket viewing at the funeral home, followed by a memorial service at East Valley Bible Church. My son's remains would then be cremated. It sounds so cold. This was my son's body. The body that I held close so many times when he was little and hugged every chance I got. The body I laid next to all night when he was little after he'd swallowed two pennies.

I was not in favor of an open casket memorial, or a viewing, for that matter. Maybe it was because I had been to open casket services for both of my grandfathers. To this day, I have not forgotten the sight of my grandfathers— the guys who loved to tease me and take me fishing— lying in a casket. In both cases, it was a sight I have never forgotten. I would have preferred to remember them only in life.

I could not bear the thought of Kevin lying in a casket. At the viewing before the memorial, I spent all of my time outside visiting with friends and family. I spent some time visiting with the mother of one of Kevin's best friends, Keith. We talked a lot about what Kevin was like. Somehow we got on the subject of procrastination. Kevin was an absolute expert at making excuses up when there was something I needed him to do that he didn't want to do. If someone else needed help with something, Kevin was always the first to volunteer, but if I needed him to clean the bathroom, or vacuum the house, or mow the grass, well, good luck with that. I told his friend's mother this and she looked at me and very matter of factly said, "Well, I guess he didn't procrastinate at everything." I asked her what she meant by that. She said, "I guess he finished his work here on earth before us." A few weeks later I wrote the following poem as I reflected on that conversation.

I Didn't Know You Were Ready

When your mother told me it was
time for you to be born
I didn't know you were ready
You learned to walk and talk before
we knew it
You learned to ride a trike
You learned to ride a bike
Soon it was time for school
I didn't know you were ready
You became a man everyone loved
You touched all you knew
Soon you had a license to drive
I didn't know you were ready
Soon you told me it was time to go
hunting
We took the class because
I didn't know you were ready
School never came easy
But you made it work
Showing everyone your heart
High school is over and life began
I didn't know you were ready

The Lord said you were ready
He said He needed you
But you didn't get to say goodbye
You came back to say goodbye
because
I didn't know you were ready

On one of Kevin's camping trips with friends, they listened to the Big and Rich album, *Horse of a Different Color*. The last song on the album is "Live this Life." When Kevin heard it, he said that if anything were to happen to him, he wanted this song played at his memorial. We opened his memorial with "Live this Life."

I mentioned earlier that on the Father's Day just three weeks before Kevin passed away, the kids had taken a jar and written down their favorite memories of me on little pieces of colored paper and put them in the jar. We read them together on Father's Day. I thought this was a neat gift, so at Kevin's memorial we asked everyone to share their favorite memories of Kevin. I certainly didn't know—and I don't think Kevin knew—how many lives he touched. We received numerous stories of how helpful, kind, and polite he was. I sometimes wondered if they were talking about the same Kevin.

I was asked if I wanted to speak at Kevin's memorial. The very thought of speaking at my son's memorial made me go weak in the knees. First of all, while I don't like to admit it, I was pretty much a basket case. No, check that; I was a basket case. Kevin's death had taken all of us by surprise and my thoughts were still a bit hazy. I wasn't sure I would have anything to say that would make any sense, or if I could even get through it if I did. I knew that there were many things I wanted to say about Kevin, but getting those words out would not be easy, to say the least.

I had never really done any public speaking. Occasionally, I would have to make a presentation at work, to a few engineers, but this was different. Getting up in front of what was expected to be a few hundred people and talking about my son who had just died was not exactly at the top of my list of things I wanted to do. I honestly didn't know if I could pull it off—and more importantly, what would I say? This wasn't about me, it was about Kevin. Somewhere in the back of my mind, I could here Kevin say, "Dad, cowboy up." I decided to speak.

I did the only thing I knew how to do. I started writing down word for word what I wanted to say. I actually read it to those who were at the house prior to the memorial. Below is an excerpt from what I said:

> Kevin was always there if someone really needed him. In elementary and junior high he had a reputation of befriending challenged kids. One of the kids he befriended was in a wheelchair. David had some problems with his legs. I am not sure what they were, but because he was in a wheelchair it was difficult for him to make friends. Kevin didn't care. He would push David around the school in his wheelchair.
>
> David's mom would drop him off at our house. The wheelchair stayed at the front door. Kevin would drag him around or he would crawl until he was exhausted. David was filthy by the end of the day, but he had fun.
>
> As Kevin grew older, he had a habit of stopping and helping people beside the road. He would often come home and tell me about stopping and helping someone on the road, and that honestly, scared me to death.
>
> Kevin, Blake, Blake's dad Kelly and I went hunting when Kevin was in junior high. We were lucky enough to fill one deer tag. It was late when we

got back to camp and decided to stay there for the night and go back to town the next day. Kelly and I did our best to hang the deer up in a tree to keep it away from any hungry critters.

We were sitting around camp when suddenly— Crash! The deer fell out of the tree and scared the boys half to death (of course it didn't scare Kelly or I).

After we rehung the deer, Kevin was very jumpy. Every time a twig moved or a leaf rattled, Kevin would say, "What was that?" Later that night, Kevin and I climbed in the bed of a truck to sleep. After a short time, Kevin asked, "Dad, could you put your rifle back here with us?" "Yes Kevin, I will."

A short time later, "Dad, do you have any shells in the magazine of your rifle?" "No Kevin, I don't, but I will put a couple of shells in." A few minutes later, "Dad, could you put one in the chamber?" "Kevin, go to sleep!"

Many of you have asked, "What can I do to help?" Well, here is what you can do.

Each of you can make "something very good" come from this. I don't know if it's one "something very good" or a thousand "something very goods." It might be a tiny "something very good" or a huge "something very good." But I am convinced that "something very good" can come from this. I don't know who, what, when, where or how, but I know that it will.

I ask each of you to find that "something very good" and make it happen. That is what you can do for us and for Kevin.

Kevin, I'll see you on the other side.

Below are some excerpts from others who spoke, along with my comments.

Our neighbor, Dwaynn, lived just west of us and had

several mules and hunting dogs. Dwaynn and I spoke often, as neighbors do. Kevin wanted to get to know him and hopefully get a chance to ride his mules. He would ask me to go over to talk to Dwaynn with him, but I wouldn't. I thought if he wanted to get to know him, he could go himself. Eventually, Kevin worked up the courage to go talk to him. It was the beginning of a very good friendship. Kevin would often go hang out with Dwaynn.

During the construction of a house between our house and Dwaynn's, there was a port-a-potty for the construction workers in the front yard. One day I was out front and saw Kevin come out of the port-a-potty and walk home. He said he had to "go" and couldn't wait another 50 yards until he got home. Kids!

Below is what Dwaynn said at Kevin's memorial:

> Kevin and I often went riding my mules up in the mountains chasing lions and bobcats with my hounds.
>
> Kevin often spoke of his family when we were out riding. He talked about his family being the most important thing to him and that he considered his dad to be his best friend.
>
> There was a noticeable change in him when he came back from riding the mules. He was very relaxed.
>
> On one of our trips, I brought along a young mule. We had just unloaded the mules when Kevin decided to get on that young mule and make sure all the gear was in order before we took off.
>
> I heard a commotion, I turned around and all I saw was dust and a cowboy hat. The young mule had spooked. Kevin finally got the mule stopped and came back to the truck to tell me what happened. I laughed and said, "By the way, it looks like your canteen is leaking because your pants are

wet." Kevin said, "That isn't because my canteen is leaking."

Kevin riding Dwaynn's mule.

Many months before Kevin passed away, Dwaynn and I were talking and the subject of Kevin came up. He said that Kevin had a pretty good head on his shoulders. He told me that he had been brought up right and that Kevin knew right from wrong. He said that this doesn't guarantee he will never do anything wrong, but he is a good kid and he does know right from wrong.

Sometime after Kevin passed away, I was going through his things and came across an assignment he had in school. One of the questions on the paper asked, "Who is your hero and why?" Kevin's response was, "My Dad

is my hero because he has taught me right from wrong."
Kevin's hero misses him very much.

Kevin's friend, Blake, said the following:

> I remember the day I met Kevin. I walked into
> class with my lunch box and saw an empty seat next
> to Kevin. I asked him if the seat next to him was
> taken. He said no and I sat down next to this kid
> with bleach blond hair and a bowl cut. He invited
> me over to his house that night to play tetherball.
>
> My favorite memory of Kevin involves a
> tootsie roll. We were at my house; both hungry and
> I had only one tootsie roll so we agreed to share it.
> I unwrapped it and set it on the counter, turned
> my head for two seconds to get a knife, I turned
> around to see Kevin chewing on the whole tootsie
> roll. I have never forgiven him for eating my half of
> the tootsie roll.
>
> I hurt my wrist and had to have surgery. Kevin
> stayed with me for a whole week after my surgery,
> keeping me company and wrapping my arm in
> plastic so I could take a shower.
>
> One night we stayed up until 3:00 a.m.
> watching movies. We were hungry and decided to
> bake a chocolate cake. We sat down to eat a piece
> of chocolate cake with a big glass of milk. That is
> when we discovered that we didn't know how to
> crack eggs very well. Let's just say the chocolate
> cake was crunchy.
>
> We took Kevin out water skiing many times.
> It seemed like we spent hours trying to get Kevin
> up on the water skis. That kid never did get up. He
> would always let go of the rope too soon.
>
> He was like a brother to me. He is my blood
> brother.

The only thing I would add to what Blake said is that

they acted like brothers most of the time—they loved to argue.

Blake's dad, Kelly:

> From the time Blake and Kevin met, Kevin always went on family vacations with us. Kevin loved going to Idaho and seeing the farms and ranches. He loved it.
>
> I relied on Kevin to keep Blake out of trouble and he did a pretty good job of it.
>
> I loved him like he was one of my sons. My only regret is that although I had many chances to tell him I loved him, I never did.
>
> I am looking forward to still going hunting with his dad because I know that is what Kevin would have wanted.

Kelly, Blake, and I do indeed still go hunting together. Kevin's friend, Trevor:

> My favorite story about Kevin was when we went on a camping trip to Queen Valley for three days. We were hanging out riding the quads and checking out a nearby cave. On one ride, I saw Kevin jump up on the side of his quad and then stop. I pulled up next to him to see what was wrong. He said a rattlesnake had just struck at him. I pulled out my .22 caliber pistol and emptied two clips into the bush where the snake was. I am not sure if I ever hit it, but Kevin was so happy that I was protecting him.
>
> Kevin loved to tell that story over and over. His girlfriend at the time said that he told it to her at least three times.
>
> What Kevin's dad said about helping others beside the road was true. We often stopped and helped others who were broke down beside the

road. We figured that if we did, someone would stop and help us if we needed it.

Kevin loved to laugh and tell a good story.

The memorial was a time to feel the support and love of friends and family. I have often been told, "God will never give you a challenge you can't handle." Well, maybe God has me mixed up with some devout religious person who can quote Bible chapter and verse for everything. God can give this challenge to someone who wants it and give me back my son. The weeks and months following Kevin's death were very difficult. I'm glad I didn't know what I was in for.

Chapter 8

My "Something Very Good"

Since the moment I heard the phrase "something very good will come from this," I have struggled with what my "something very good" is.

I thought maybe I should email a local paper and see if I could get a columnist to write an editorial about the problems with alcohol. I guess I was hoping they would write some magical editorial that would make this all okay for me and maybe prevent this type of tragedy from happening again. I sent a letter to E.J. Montini at the Arizona Republic newspaper explaining what had happened to my son. I told him that I was hoping maybe there was "something very good" he could do. As fate would have it, he never answered my letter.

I wrote many poems and a few editorials for local papers, trying to make sense of what I was feeling. I often found myself reflecting on how I had gotten to this point in my life. I wondered about Kevin, where he was, and what his life might have been like had he survived that night. Would he have settled down with a nice girl, had babies, and lived the life I wanted him to? Maybe he would have settled down close by and we could have continued our close father/son relationship, and—most importantly—I would go before him, as it should be.

I also emailed some of the school faculty where Kevin attended high school. I was hoping they could have their students write papers about the problems with alcohol. Here is what I asked.

1. Why do people go out and drink excessively or do drugs?

2. If you were given the opportunity to solve the problem of excessive drinking and drug use (you are in charge) and you had unlimited resources (money and time), how would you solve this problem?

3. If you could go out and do anything you want (you have unlimited resources, i.e. money), what would you do and why?

I believe that first we must understand "why" before we can fix anything. I also believe that the younger you are, the more you look at the world without paradigms. I suspect that the solutions to many of our problems are right in front of us and we can't see them. We need a fresh set of young eyes.

As you can see from the above, I was struggling with the "why" and hoping to get some feedback on how to prevent these types of tragedies from recurring. I still believe that we must focus on prevention at a very early age. The analogy I like to give is that you walk into a house and you see water spraying everywhere from a broken pipe and there are many people in the house all trying to mop up the water, but no one is trying to shut off the water. We need to find a way to "shut off the water," so to speak.

The idea to speak and tell the story about what happened to Kevin didn't really occur to me until maybe two months after he died. I had no clue what this "something very good" might be and I still don't, but I intend to do my best to figure it out.

I spoke at a local juvenile detention center. I really had no clue what I was doing, but I knew I had to start somewhere. I expanded somewhat on what I'd said at Kevin's memorial. I wanted everyone who heard me speak to know what it felt like to lose a child. I think the students understood my point. I received many nice letters from them.

As I reflect back on this, perhaps I should have waited a little longer before I started speaking publicly. In the beginning, it was very difficult. I would start to cry and have to stop and compose myself. Even today, I will have moments when it's very difficult. One particularly difficult moment came when I was speaking to a group of young adults that had been arrested for being in possession of alcohol. At the end of my presentation, time permitting, I usually select a few poems and read them. A few days prior to this, I had written something I call "A Letter from Heaven."

Dear Dad,

First, I would like to say how much I miss you and I love you. I am sorry about what happened; you have no idea how sorry. We were just out having a good time. I didn't think anyone could get hurt. It seemed so fun and everyone was doing it.

One minute we were drinking and having a good time and the next minute I was dead. I want you to know how hard I tried to live; how much I wanted to go back to the beginning of that night and change it all.

I never believed it could ever happen to me. I knew people who had problems with alcohol, but I wasn't one of *them*, I knew better. I saw other people do it and get away with it, so I figured I could also.

I had so much left to do, Dad. My life was just starting. I was looking forward to coming home and raiding the refrigerator and the pantry. I was looking forward to many more hunting trips, working on the old yellow truck together, getting married, and giving you more grandchildren. I was looking forward to spoiling Collin and Trinity, and complaining about having to help my sisters all the time.

I will never get to share Thanksgiving dinner or Christmas with you again. No more gifts, no more falling asleep after Thanksgiving dinner, no more giving each other haircuts, no more arguing about who lost what tool.

You have so many pictures of me around the house. I know what I did caused everyone great sadness. I know about what you plan to do. I will be with you every step of the way. I can't believe how many people are helping you and how anxious they are to help. Tell them all I said thank you.

Tell everyone you can about what happened to me. Tell them how dangerous alcohol abuse can be and how it only takes once for terrible things to happen. Tell all the kids that what can happen is not cool and that it can happen to them.

Tell them about the pain it brings to family and friends. Tell them so they don't have to find out the hard way, the way I did.

Something very good will come from this, Dad. I just wish I were there to share it with you. I love you and miss you.

> Your son,
> Kevin

I had never read "A Letter from Heaven" out loud (big mistake) prior to speaking to this group. As I started to read it, I started crying, and I was having trouble composing myself. Bev was sitting in the back of the room. I glanced back at her— no help there. I could see she was crying, too. For the most part though, telling Kevin's story has been very therapeutic for me. Many people have said that telling this story must be very difficult and at times that is true. But when students come up and thank me for speaking to them, I always wonder if maybe this is the "something very good" Kevin spoke of. Will I ever know what my "something very good" is?

Chapter 9

The Idea

As one might imagine, we struggled with what to do with Kevin's ashes. The funeral home called to let me know Kevin's body had been cremated. I immediately went to pick up his ashes. I put them in the front passenger seat next to me and started the car. I picked the ashes up, held them close, and started crying. This was as close as I was ever going to get to giving Kevin one last hug. I decided to take Kevin for one last ride past the places where he grew up. I drove past the house he'd lived in for 12 years, his elementary school, his junior high, and his high school, and down the same streets he'd walked and rode his bike to school-where he'd lived his life.

I wrote this poem after I went to pick up Kevin's ashes. I thought about all the things I had been through lately and thought, *I wouldn't wish this on my worst enemy.*

I Hope

I hope you never pick out your son's casket

I hope you never have to tell your daughters that their brother is gone

I hope you never have to decide whether to cremate or bury your son

I hope you never have to pick the songs for your son's memorial

I hope you never have to pick the pictures for your son's memorial video

I hope you never have to go pick up your son's ashes

I hope you never have to go pick up your son's death certificates

I hope you never have to prepare to speak at your son's memorial

I hope you never have to read your son's obituary

I hope you hug your children everyday

I hope you cherish every day you have with them

I hope what is important is now very clear

I hope you hold all who are dear very close to your heart

I hope you find your joy and purpose in life

I hope you find a way to make your dreams come true

We had talked about leaving his ashes up in northern Arizona where Kevin shot his first and only elk. Kevin and I did a lot of things together. We played golf together, we worked on vehicles together, we gave each other haircuts, and we went hunting together. Before he was going to go hunting, we decided he needed to take a hunters' safety course. Of course, Kevin decided that I had to take it with him. I found it to be very educational and I highly recommend it to anyone who's going to go hunting. It's worthwhile for anyone who spends time outdoors. It's filled with good information about gun safety and what to do if you ever get lost in the woods.

In the fall of 2004, we were all lucky enough to be drawn to go elk hunting. In Arizona, it can be difficult to get drawn for rifle elk hunting, with many years in between draws for good areas. This was the first time Kelly and I had been drawn to go elk hunting with our sons. At the time, we talked about how this might be the trip of a lifetime.

The area we were drawn for is high mountain area in northeastern Arizona, covered with towering ponderosa pine trees. Kevin was 17 years old at the time. The hunting party included my brother Lark and his son, Josh, Kevin's best friend Blake, Blake's dad Kelly, Kevin, and me. We scouted the area several times. Each time we were up there, we saw elk. One of the scouting trips was to an area where no motorized vehicles were allowed. We—or more accurately, I—decided to hike. Kevin and I hiked several miles into this area. As usual, Kevin complained about all the walking and kept telling me we shouldn't have to hike this far to hunt. As we made our way back, we saw a flock of wild turkeys and several elk. When we got to the truck, Kevin agreed that maybe getting off the road was a good idea, even though he still didn't like the idea of hiking.

On another scouting trip with Kelly and Blake, I remember stopping at the only gas station in a tiny town for gas and snacks. The boys decided they wanted some burritos and hot dogs. Keep in mind these burritos and hotdogs are kept warm in an oven together. Blake decided that his burrito tasted like a hot dog and Kevin decided that his hot dog tasted like a burrito. I think we have all had that experience. There's nothing quite like a gas station burrito to get your stomach churning.

Leading up to the hunt, I had several discussions with Kevin about how many days he was going to be allowed to take off from school and that his grades were going to play a major part in that decision. Oddly enough, Kevin kept his grades up pretty well that fall.

Packing for a hunting trip like this can be an ordeal, but Kevin was very anxious to get going, so he was a huge help. I think he packed most of the truck himself. One of the things Kevin always worried about on hunting and camping trips was toilet paper. He once told me that we needed one roll of toilet paper per day, per person, on hunting and camping trips. I used to rib him pretty hard about it. It seemed like everywhere I looked in the truck, there was a roll of toilet paper-kids. I went through Kevin's room one day after he passed away and it seemed that in every backpack he had there was a roll of toilet paper.

We didn't exactly rough it on this hunting trip. My brother had a friend with a cabin very close to the area we were hunting, so we had a nice warm cabin and a hot shower to come home to each night. While hunting was important, enjoying the hunt was more important.

We spent a great deal of time deciding what we would eat. The menu usually included homemade split-pea soup, chili, cinnamon rolls, cookies, and plenty of munchies.

Normally by mid-November there is quite a bit of snow in this area, but that year there was no snow. The air was brisk and clean, but not particularly cold.

The first couple of days went by uneventfully. Each day, we left the cabin well before daylight and returned after dark. On Saturday, the third day of the hunt, we went back to hunt in the same area we had been hunting in for the first two days. We hadn't seen any elk, but there was quite a bit of evidence that there were elk in the area. Besides, it was a fun area to hike and hang around in.

We had a typical way that we hunted. This involved dropping two hunters off up on top of a ridge, and then they would hunt down the ridge. A third person would drive down to a predetermined place and wait for them. On this day, the weather was clear and cool. The air was fresh with the smell of fall. My brother Lark and Kevin decided to hunt down a ridge that was covered with huge ponderosa pine and at an elevation of approximately 7,500 feet.

My nephew, Josh, and I would drive down to the bottom of the ridge and wait for them. We dropped Lark and Kevin off mid-afternoon and then drove down to the bottom to wait. After a couple of hours, I heard a gun shot, and then another, and then another. Kevin was hunting with my 30.06 rifle and I was very familiar with the sound. I was pretty sure that it was a 30.06 I heard, and it seemed to be about the right distance away, but it could have been another hunter in the area. I tried not to get my hopes up too high. I sat and waited patiently. It seemed like an eternity, but it probably wasn't too much longer that my brother Lark showed up without Kevin; hmm, probably a good sign.

Lark said that they had come across several elk just after they left the truck. As they made their way down the ridge, they lost all sign of the elk. They stopped to talk about what to do next, when one jumped up 50 yards behind Kevin. Lark said, "Elk." Kevin spun around and fired off a shot. The elk took off running down the ridge. They walked over to where they last saw the elk and saw the elk Kevin shot at maybe 40 yards away. Kevin fired two more times and the elk just stood there. The elk took a few more steps and dropped. Kevin looked like he was going to do a victory dance with the rifle in hand. Lark grabbed the barrel, pointed it towards the ground, and they stood there grinning at each other. I am sure this was a very special moment for Kevin and his uncle Lark. In hindsight, I wish I could have also been there to see Kevin's face and hear the excitement in his voice when he dropped the elk.

As I mentioned earlier, we usually hunted in pairs. The reason being that when you are successful, one hunter can stay with the animal while the other one goes for help. Processing an animal this large is a major project.

Before they had gone, I'd given Lark my GPS unit and explained to him how to mark the spot in case they were successful. Lark had dutifully marked the spot and we are lucky he did. We only had an hour of daylight left and the route he had taken to get to the truck took him quite a while. We decided to drive up the road and see how close we could get to the spot on the road. It turned out that they were less than a half a mile from the road.

We loaded up a wagon that we had purchased for just this type of thing with flashlights, lanterns, rope, saws, etc. Next, we headed into the woods to find Kevin. When we started getting close, I yelled for Kevin and he answered with a very excited hoop and holler. I will never forget how excited he sounded as he guided us toward him. When we got there, he was smiling ear to ear. I would venture to guess that this was probably his proudest moment, bagging an elk at the age of 17. The truth be told, I am 50 years old, and have hunted elk for many years, but I've never been successful. It was a very proud moment for me also.

I had often warned Kevin that all the fun stops after you shoot something. That is when the work begins. This was no exception. Kevin experienced the joy of bagging his first and, as it would turn out, only elk. I made it clear from the time we found him that he was going to dress this animal (with my guidance). He never complained about it once and followed my instructions very carefully. By the time we got the elk on the wagon and headed for the truck, there was not much light left in the day. In fact, it was very dark by the time we made it back to the truck. Kevin didn't stop talking all the way back to the cabin. He couldn't wait to get back there and tell his friend Blake all about it. Kevin had instantly become "The Great Hunter" and had all kinds of advice for us and Blake. Although I don't recall specifically, I'm thinking Kevin didn't sleep a wink that night.

Often I will reflect back on this adventure; I'm glad that I was able to be there with Kevin. At the time, I remember thinking about how many more times like this we would have and maybe someday, God willing, Kevin would do the same things with his son.

Hunting trips will never be quite the same without Kevin, but I also know that he would want me to continue the tradition. Perhaps one day, good Lord willin', I will have the opportunity to take my grandsons on a hunting trip.

One of my thoughts about where to spread Kevin's ashes was in the area where Kevin got his elk, as it was a very proud and joyous moment for him. I did give it very serious consideration. In the beginning, I was very torn about what Kevin would have wanted.

I grew up in Kalispell, Montana. Kevin loved it up there. We went up there on vacation several times and I believe that some of Kevin's happiest times were in Montana. On Kevin's first trip to Montana, he got to meet my uncle, R.T., who is a pilot. R.T. offered to take him flying with one condition: Kevin would have to remove his earring that he wore at the time. It turned out the earring was stuck in his ear and was very painful to remove. The earring was finally removed successfully and Kevin ended up going flying with R.T. many times. Kevin never put the earring back in. He did turn the tables on R.T. by asking him to show him how to polish his boots. R.T. spent a couple of hours showing him how to do it. To my knowledge, Kevin never shined his boots again.

While in Montana, Kevin went flying with his uncle, went fishing, and went on several float trips down the middle fork of the Flathead River. He spoke often of wanting to move to Montana someday and buy a ranch. Kevin also wanted us to build a house up there so he could go up and housesit for us.

Kevin's friend, Blake, suggested that maybe we should take Kevin's ashes to Montana. I liked the idea of taking his ashes to Montana. The downside of this was that his ashes would not be nearby and we could not go visit them easily, but I felt like this was where he would want to be laid to rest.

Kevin loved to watch westerns. One of his favorite westerns was the movie, *Lonesome Dove*. When I told him about it, he wasn't all that interested in watching it, as it was a very long movie lasting over four hours. Once he started watching it, he really enjoyed it and watched almost the entire movie in one night.

In that movie, the character played by Tommy Lee Jones agrees to carry the body of Robert Duvall back to Texas from Montana on horseback to be buried where he was the happiest.

A few days after Blake suggested we take Kevin's ashes to Montana, the idea to walk occurred to me. I was standing in our circa 1980s kitchen, leaned up against the stove. I knew at that moment what I was going to do and quite frankly, I didn't care what anyone thought of it. I was going to put Kevin's ashes in my backpack and walk to Montana with them.

It has been said that "God chooses the unimpressive to do His work." I guess I have to admit, I fall in to the "unimpressive" category, but I wish so desparately that He could have given me an assignment like organizing a raffle or bake sale.

I walked into the next room where my wife, Bev, was doing something on the computer. I told her I knew what I wanted to do with Kevin's ashes. She walked over to me, hugged me, and we both started crying. We stood there hugging and crying for quite a while. I don't recall what she said, but I knew that she would support whatever I wanted to do. My first vision of what this might be like was not exactly what it turned out to be. I envisioned Bev and me taking off with the truck and a camper on the back and honestly, I didn't expect very many people would even know I was gone—sort of like Forrest Gump. The idea to stop and share the story about what happened to Kevin is something I had thought about, but at the time I wasn't sure that I would do it. As it turned out, it became a major part of the walk. Boy, am I glad I can be flexible.

Initially, I thought that maybe I would walk along the Continental Divide. I started doing some research and discovered that this would be very tough to do. It's over 3,000 miles to Montana going along the Continental Divide Trail, best I could tell. The Continental Divide Trail would be a very difficult hike. Obviously, this route would preclude me from stopping and telling the story of Kevin.

I decided that it would be best to stick to the roads. This would allow for plenty of support along the way. Admittedly, in *Lonesome Dove*, Tommy Lee Jones did it on horseback, but I'm not exactly a cowboy, and riding a horse from Gilbert, Arizona to Kalispell, Montana seemed to have many challenges (i.e. a recipe for disaster) that I didn't think I could deal with, not the least of which would be a few saddle sores. In the end, I think I made the right decision.

When we told our children about our plans, they all talked about wanting to go along. For various reasons, Sarah and her boyfriend, Ed, were the only others that came along. They alternated days with me on the road.

I did some research on the Internet and found out about a guy by the name of Ray who had ridden his bike from Phoenix to Ground Zero. It turns out that he lived in Gilbert. I sent him an email and told him briefly what I wanted to do. To my surprise, he answered my email and agreed to get together with me and answer questions I had about how he made his trip. We got together at a coffee shop in Gilbert in September of 2005. I wasn't sure what to expect. I had so many questions and not the foggiest notion as to how to pull off something like this.

Ray was very friendly and helpful. We talked a great deal about the complexities of a cross-country journey on foot. By now I had been considering stopping along the way and sharing the story of Kevin.

Ray told me about his trip and the day-to-day details. He also talked about how he stopped along the way to speak to different organizations. After hearing Ray describe how he enjoyed this part of his trip, I thought that I should also do this.

I think it was clear to him that I was very concerned about how I was going to be able to accomplish this feat. Ray said a couple things to me that had a major impact on my perspective of this walk. He said, "You can't do this alone. You're going to need to get an organization behind you to help you set this up." Secondly, and more importantly, he said, "How do you think you'll feel about it in ten years if you don't do this?" Those words really hit home with me and I will always be grateful to him. I realized that an opportunity like this to help others would probably never pass my way again. How could I not do this?

Ray left me with one warning. He told me that I needed to understand that not everyone would think this was a great idea. He told me that my relatives would be among those who discouraged the idea. As it turned out, Ray was correct.

Several well-meaning people did their best to convince

me not to do this or to change it in a way that I was not comfortable with. Most of these discussions were polite and well intentioned, but some were a bit, shall we say, "heated." I think that most of the concern was about my ability to complete this journey. Most of these people were probably concerned that I would fail. Looking back on it, I can't blame anyone for thinking that way.

Just who did I think I was? A gifted athlete? Not hardly. Was I an experienced manager? Nope; I've gone out of my way in my career not to manage. Any contacts in the non-profit/ philanthropy world? Not a one. Could I afford to take many months off work? Not exactly. Am I a good salesman and a leader who could convince others that this was a good idea? Yeah, right.

I started thinking of those who might be able to help me with this walk.

Chapter 10

The Search for Help

It's a funny and sad thing when you lose a child; sometimes doors are opened to you just because you've lost a child. I found this to be true over and over. People just seemed to be willing to listen to what I had to say.

What kind of organization would be willing to take on such a project? Did I want a large organization? A small organization? Or, more importantly, would I find any organization that would help? If I stood back and looked at it objectively and was honest with myself, it would be a major risk for any organization to commit resources to the walk, and why would they do it? How would complete strangers know if I had what it took to succeed? This was something that, as far as I knew, had not been done. So what criteria would I use? Would I find an organization with a "Long Walk and Talk Coordinator" on their payroll? The only reason any organization would help is because they believed in doing the right thing and had the ability to trust.

I sent letters and made phone calls to numerous organizations. I waited patiently—okay, maybe impatiently—for the phone to ring. Those letters and phone calls went unanswered. I began to wonder if I was the only one that thought this was a good idea. Well, of course my blushing bride thought it was a good idea, also.

In the fall of 2005 I contacted SADD (Students Against Destructive Decisions). SADD's mission is to provide students with the best prevention tools possible to deal with the issues of underage drinking, drug use, impaired driving, and other destructive decisions.

I asked them if they were looking for speakers. They told me that they were and that I should come to one of their meetings to hear someone else speak to see if it looked like a fit for me. Bev and I decided we would go.

At this meeting, SADD had a speaker by the name of Jim Walker who had lost his 17-year-old son to a drunk driver. The drunk driver was a 21-year-old kid that by Jim's own description was a "good kid." He had dropped out of school at 16 to support his mother and younger sister. He had just received his GED (General Equivalency Diploma) and was in the process of joining the Marine Corps. But this 21-year-old went out one night and got drunk, got behind the wheel of a car, and killed Jim's son. He's now sitting in prison and will be there for quite a while, all because of one night, one careless, stupid night—a night that changed his life, his family's life, and Jim's life in an instant.

When Jim was finished speaking, we went up and introduced ourselves. Jim was very kind and we chatted for several minutes. I told him about how I wanted to start speaking and telling the story about what happened to Kevin. He told me about notMYkid. NotMYkid is an organization that empowers youth to reach their full potential by inspiring positive life choices. He said he had been speaking for them and that they were looking for speakers.

After talking with Jim, I decided to contact notMYkid and see if they had any interest in using me as a speaker and maybe, just maybe, my little adventure I had planned. To my surprise, after sending them an email, I received a phone call from a young lady by the name of Christina. Little did I know at the time that she would become my mentor and help me to understand the importance of what I was doing.

We met at a coffee shop in downtown Phoenix. I thought we were going to visit for a little while and see if I was a fit for their organization. I was surprised when Christina asked me to tell my story to her right there and then. I can safely say I didn't do a very good job of telling her about what happened to Kevin. Christina sat quietly and listened. I also told her about the idea I was kicking around regarding walking to Montana with Kevin's ashes and sharing our story along the way. Once again, Christina just sat quietly and listened. She really didn't say much. I'm not sure what I really expected her to say, but I thought she would give me some feedback. I didn't have any idea what she thought about it. When we said goodbye, I felt like maybe she decided this wasn't a good fit. I wasn't sure I would ever hear from her again. When I got in the car, I called Bev to let her know I was on my way home. She asked me how it went and I told her I wasn't too sure.

As I drove home I reflected on my conversation with Christina. I had this nagging feeling that it had not gone well. I began to seriously question my ability to convince anyone that this was a good idea. Deep down, I knew this was a good idea; I just needed to come up with a better way of convincing others. The problem wasn't with the idea; it was with me. I guess it's fairly obvious that I don't take rejection all that well.

Little did I know that Christina was hooked from the beginning. Christina and I would talk many times in the coming months about that day. I told her I never wanted to play poker with her because I never had the foggiest notion what she was thinking.

As it turned out, notMYkid, founded by Dr. Mark Rohde, and Debbie and Steve Moak, was the first organization that demonstrated interest in supporting my walk to Montana with Kevin's ashes. NotMYkid jumped in and did nothing short of an incredible job building support for this effort. I will always be very thankful to them for their efforts. Without notMYkid, I am not sure I would have been able to make this walk happen.

Now all we had to do was figure out how to make this happen.

Chapter 11

Planning for a Long Walk

There were a thousand places I could go wrong with the planning. I could get sick, I could get hurt, or I could lose a lot of time because of bad weather.

The only thing I had going for me was my stubbornness. I was simply a dude who'd lost his son and wanted to make "something very good" come from it. I never wavered in my belief that I could make it happen. I understood that it was a huge undertaking that was going to require a large amount of support from complete strangers. But as Ray said, "How do you think you will feel about it in ten years if you don't do it?" In hindsight, I'm glad I didn't know what it was going to take and how many lucky breaks I was going to need. I always say, "I would rather be lucky than good any day."

I guess if you truly believe in something, you'll find a way to make it happen, and that is just what we did. I often hear young adults talk about how they want to stay clean, but they cave in to peer pressure. Here is the way I like to look at it: If I told you I would give you a million dollars if you would stay clean until you were 21, could you do it?

I came across this quote and I think it describes my thought process best.

> "Far better it is to dare mighty things, to win glorious triumphs, even though checkered by failure, than to rank with those poor spirits who neither enjoy much nor suffer much, because they live in a gray twilight that knows not victory nor defeat."
>
> Theodore Roosevelt

I will be the first to admit that I probably came close to driving Bev crazy with the planning, although I would argue it's a short trip for her. She has to be a bit off her rocker to put up with a guy like me. We talked about it constantly. Maybe more accurately, I fretted about how I was going to make it happen. There seemed to be thousands of details to worry about and I found myself thinking about it all the time.

Chapter 12

When to Leave

One of the first questions I had to answer was when to leave. I wanted to be sure that I did most of the walk during the school year. If I walked during the summer, most schools would be out, so this would greatly limit the number of speaking opportunities. Departing late spring or early summer would be the simplest from a weather perspective. I would have to deal with the heat, but I would not have to worry too much about getting snowed in somewhere. If I left in the early fall, the further I walked, the worse the weather could get. I would probably be finishing close to Christmas time. Walking along the snow covered highways of Montana in December seemed like a recipe for disaster.

I came to the conclusion that leaving in the February timeframe made the most sense. At this point, it was late in the fall of 2005 and I didn't know if we could be ready to leave by February of 2006.

This meant waiting until February of 2007. This also meant that we were at least 16 months from leaving. At the time, I felt like this was too long of a wait and maybe I was overestimating what needed to be accomplished before we left. I would have really liked to have left in 2006, but in hindsight, I am glad I didn't. As I discovered later, it takes a lot of time to plan something like this out (well, at least it does for a dude like me).

In one of the early planning meetings at notMYkid, it became clear to me that I was going to have to settle on a date and stick with it. We decided that it would be meaningful to leave Arizona on or near what would have been Kevin's 20th birthday. Kevin was born on February 26th. We decided to leave on February 24th.

Chapter 13

Schedule for the Walk

Scheduling the walk was another subject that I pondered a great deal. If notMYkid was going to schedule speaking engagements along the way, I had to come up with a schedule I could keep. I also understood that time is money and the longer I took to get to Montana, the more it would cost.

I did as much research as I could about other individuals who had done things kind of like this. I read about guys who ran across the country and averaged almost 200 miles a week. Studs, indeed. I also read about people who walked across the country and ran into health problems that greatly slowed down their progress.

Along with guessing how many miles a week I could walk, I had to plan time for an unknown number of speaking engagements. As I mentioned earlier, I also had to plan for possible bad weather days that would prevent me from walking.

I would like to claim that I did a few cool, calm calculations and very scientifically decided how long it would take, but that would be something less than the truth. My best guess was that I could average 90 miles a week if all went well.

It also became clear that I had to set a date for when I would complete this journey, so that plans could be made for a finale. We decided that it would be meaningful to finish the walk near the second anniversary of Kevin's death. Kevin died on July 10th, so we settled on July 1st, which was a Sunday. At 90 miles a week, this would leave roughly 2 weeks for weather, illness, or injury.

I completely understand that the start and stop of this walk were symbolic, but they did mean a lot to me and I hoped Kevin approved. As I went through this process, I thought a lot about what Kevin might say if he were here. As our children grow up, they often seek our approval. For me, the tables were turned and I did my best to do things in a way that I thought Kevin would approve of.

Along with the start and stop dates, we had to give this walk a name. NotMYkid was very gracious and also adamant that it needed to be a name I liked. We threw several ideas out, most of which had my name in them, but as I have said from the beginning, this walk was not about me, it was about Kevin. This would be Kevin's journey to his final resting place. It seemed like it had to have walking and Kevin's name in it. The first time I said it, I started crying. Kevin's Last Walk. Debbie and Pam looked at me in stunned silence. They both agreed that we would call it Kevin's Last Walk. From that moment on, that is what we called it.

Chapter 14

Incredible Donations

NotMYkid had verbally agreed to support Kevin's Last Walk, but had not determined how it would be funded. In June of 2006, Debbie Moak invited me to speak at a notMYkid Board of Directors meeting. As usual, I asked how much time I had to speak, which is always a good thing to know. Unfortunately, there was a slight misunderstanding about how much time I had. I thought I had 20 to 25 minutes to tell Kevin's story. When Bev and I arrived, I found out I had 5 minutes. I sat there thinking, how do I convince a bunch of strangers that Kevin's Last Walk will be good for notMYkid? What could I say in five minutes that would make them believe I could indeed pull it off?

I brought a large picture of Kevin so they could put a face with the name. I set up Kevin's picture on an easel. Just before I started speaking, I decided that I would very briefly tell them what happened to Kevin. I would read a couple of poems and then I would tell them about Kevin's Last Walk. As I spoke, members of the Board of Directors sat very still and the room was very quiet. When I finished, I got up to gather Kevin's picture and the easel. Todd Stottlemyre was sitting next to me. He got up and very politely handed me Kevin's picture and the easel. He said, "Thanks for stopping by," and we shook hands.

When I walked out, Bev asked me how I thought it went, and the truth was, as usual, I wasn't sure. I was afraid it was too little time to get the Board's attention.

The next day after, I called Pam (executive director of notMYkid) to talk about how it went. I planned to apologize for not being well prepared. Pam was very excited and told me that one of the people there had volunteered to put up a good portion of the money to make this happen. That person was Todd. I started crying when she told me the good news. I think at this point, we all started to realize that Kevin's Last Walk was really coming to life.

In June of 2005, just a few weeks before Kevin passed away, I started a new job. I went to work for Rohde & Schwarz, a manufacturer of radio frequency and microwave test equipment, as an applications engineer. During the interview process, I was told more than once that Rohde & Schwarz was a very compassionate company. I remember thinking, *That's nice, but are they really?* I had no way of knowing at the time that Rohde & Schwarz America would have an opportunity to show us all what a very compassionate company they are.

As one might imagine, one of my big concerns about Kevin's Last Walk was whether I would have a job when I returned. I thought I might have enough money saved up to cover most of the expenses, but it would probably take most of my life's savings. If I didn't have a job when I returned, I would be broke and jobless.

Along the way, I did have many people inquire about my background and employment situation. They were all very surprised at the answer. No, I am not independently wealthy or retired. I had never really done any public speaking or volunteer work out of the ordinary. The extent of my volunteer work was coaching little league and flipping pancakes or burgers at church functions. I also coached many of Kevin's little league teams. It was a very busy time indeed. At one point, all three of my children were in softball and baseball. I was actually coaching two teams at the same time.

I've come to realize that many people don't test their limits or step outside their comfort zone because of money concerns. I find this very sad. I sincerely believe that everyone should have a dream and that they should do all they can to make it happen. It's very important to have a dream and to hold on to that dream. When we are very young, we often dream that some day we will grow up and be a great athlete, president, or maybe travel the world or find a cure for cancer. Hold on to those dreams. Maybe your dreams change, but never, ever stop dreaming. If a short, pudgy, old bald dude like me can pull off something like Kevin's Last Walk, imagine what you can do. As the dude says, "Dream big, it might come true."

I was out playing golf one time and I wasn't hitting the ball so well. The guy I was playing with gave me some interesting advice. He said, "Swing hard, son, in case you hit it!" Great advice in golf and in life. If you are feeling depressed, sad, or lonely, get out and help someone. I have found that by helping others, I am often helping myself.

This may be hard for some to believe, but I really do like my job. I didn't want to quit my job to do this walk, but one of the decisions that had to be made early on was whether I would allow anyone to talk me out of this. I decided that I wasn't going to let anyone talk me out of it; at least that's what I told everyone. Colin Powell said it best: "Don't let adverse facts get in the way of a good decision."

I knew that asking an employer to allow me to take four months off while I completed a walk was probably not a reasonable request. I figured that the worst that could happen would be that they would say, "Well, good luck with that, but we will fill your position when you leave." I thought a lot about what I wanted to say to them and how I might be able to convince them to hold my job for me, or perhaps maybe, just maybe, keep me on the payroll while I was walking. I put together arguments about how this would be good for Rohde & Schwarz. I also found some important statistics and a few slick arguments about helping society, etc.

The morning before I spoke to my boss and the human resources manager, I decided to stick with what had worked for me: just tell the story of Kevin and ask them to support this effort in any way they felt comfortable. Once again, I walked away without a good idea of how it was received. I dutifully called Bev and she asked the usual question, "What do you think they'll do?" I told her that I honestly had no idea.

Once again, I would be absolutely humbled and amazed at the support I would receive. Rohde & Schwarz America decided that not only would my position be waiting for me, but also they would keep me on the payroll the entire time. The way they did this was through a vacation drive. Employees could contribute their vacation time to me. The employees of Rohde & Schwarz America were incredibly generous in contributing vacation. We had more than enough hours to cover the time off that I needed. I owe a few of them a copy of this book.

The only thing my employer asked of me was to work eight hours a week so that I could keep current with new technologies and customers. My job as an applications engineer requires me to support customers in my area. If I were gone for four months, someone would have to cover for me. Prior to talking to my boss and the human resource manager, I called the applications engineers in nearby states and told them what I wanted to do and asked them if they would be willing to support this. Without hesitation, they all said yes.

I still find what Rohde & Schwarz America and my fellow employees did to be truly amazing and generous. My family and I will be forever grateful to them.

Chapter 15

Too Old to Sleep Under Bridges

This is where I have to admit that I was very stubborn and did not change my mind. At the time of this walk, I was 48 years old. I was going to be walking approximately 90 miles a week and speaking a few times a week. I had no desire whatsoever to sleep in a tent, under a bridge, or in a campground. Yes, that's right, I wanted a hot shower and a warm bed every night, so that meant hotels. I know some of you are thinking that's wimpy, and I can't argue that point. The other major advantage of the hotels was that we didn't have to worry about laundering our own sheets and towels. Bev will tell you she spent plenty of time doing laundry as it was.

Chapter 16

Routes and Schedule

Once we settled on a start and stop date, we needed to come up with a schedule and a specific route. Normally when we drive to Montana, we do a lot of driving on the freeway. I wasn't so sure I wanted to walk along the freeway for 1,400 miles. I also wanted to make sure that I took the shortest route possible for very selfish reasons. In all my trips to Montana, I never once thought about walking it. Driving 1,400 miles is painful enough, but walking? Not the sort of thought the average guy has.

So I did something I considered absolutely brilliant: I bought some maps and started looking at the possibilities. For those of you that are slightly geographically challenged, below are three maps that outline the basic route.

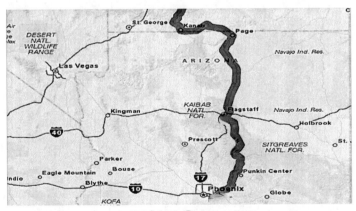

Arizona Route

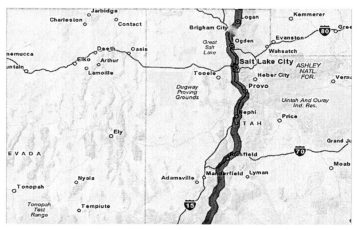

Utah Route

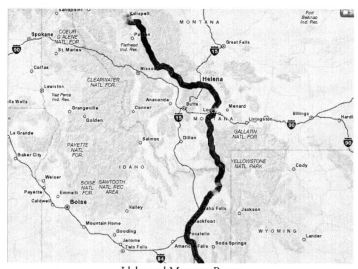

Idaho and Montana Route

It turns out that I did not take the shortest route possible through Idaho and Montana. Perhaps there are some who would say I went too far out of my way, and maybe I did, but it was the best compromise I could come up with in regards to safety, weather, freeways, and traffic.

The next little detail was to provide the dates that we

would be in each town so that notMYkid could schedule the speaking engagements. This turned out to be a very time consuming and painful process. NotMYkid could not start scheduling speaking engagements until this schedule was finalized. Below is an example of the schedule we came up with.

Mileage Between Towns/Total Mileage

Town/City	Miles from Previous Town	Total Miles	Dates in Area	# Night Stay
Gilbert, AZ	Starting Point	0	2/24 - 2/25	5
Fountain Hills, AZ	22.25	22.25	2/25 - 3/1	
Sunflower, AZ	32.67	54.92		
Payson, AZ	**32.32**	**87.24**	**3/1 - 3/6**	**5**
Strawberry, AZ	17.81	105.05	3/6 - 3/8	2
Happy Jack, AZ	34.82	139.87	3/8 - 3/10	2
Flagstaff, AZ	**43.14**	**183.01**	**3/10 - 3/16**	**6**
Cameron, AZ	51.83	234.84	3/16 - 3/18	2
Tuba City, AZ	25.57	260.41	3/18 - 3/22	4
Page, AZ	**79.69**	**340.1**	**3/22 - 3/29**	**6**
Kanab, UT	**73.14**	**413.24**	**3/29 - 4/3**	**5**
Glendale, UT	26.81	440.05	4/3 - 4/7	4
Panguitch, UT	**41.63**	**481.68**	**4/7 - 4/11**	**4**
Circleville, UT	27.63	509.31	4/11 - 4/12	
Marysville, UT	20.67	529.98	4/11 - 4/14	3
Richfield, UT	**31**	**560.98**	**4/14 - 4/18**	**4**
Salina, UT	19.59	580.57		
Gunnison, UT	14.18	594.75	4/18 - 4/21	3
Nephi, UT	**42.77**	**637.52**	**4/21 - 4/26**	**5**
Payson, UT	25.76	663.28	4/26 - 4/28	
Provo, UT	**18.35**	**681.63**	**4/26 - 4/30**	**5**
Lehi, UT	18.76	700.39		
Salt Lake City, UT	**38.44**	**738.83**	**5/1 - 5/6**	**6**

Town/City	Miles from Previous Town	Total Miles	Dates in Area	# Night Stay
Ogden, UT	**36.07**	**774.9**	**5/6 - 5/9**	3
Brigham City, UT	22.24	797.14	5/9 - 5/11	2
Logan, UT	**25.82**	**822.96**	**5/11 - 5/14**	3
Preston, ID	26.9	849.86	5/14 - 5/16	2
Downey, ID	28.68	878.54	5/16 - 5/18	2
McCammon, ID	16.41	894.95	5/18 - 5/20	2
Pocatello, ID	**25.15**	**920.1**	**5/20 - 5/23**	3
Blackfoot, ID	**24.76**	**944.86**	**5/23 - 5/25**	2
Idaho Falls, ID	**25.67**	**970.53**	**5/25 - 5/28**	3
Rexburg, ID	**30.45**	**1000.98**	**5/28 - 5/31**	3
Ashton, ID	27.74	1028.72	5/31 - 6/4	4
Island Park, ID	27.11	1055.83	6/4 - 6/6	2
Cameron, MT	62.15	1117.98	6/6 - 6/9	3
Norris, MT	27.32	1145.3	6/9 - 6/11	2
Three Forks, MT	31.64	1176.94	6/11 - 6/15	4
Townsend, MT	35.27	1212.21	6/15 - 6/18	3
Helena, MT	**34.08**	**1246.29**	**6/18 - 6/25**	7
Ovando, MT	73.89	1320.18	6/25 - 6/27	2
Seeley Lake, MT	28.52	1348.7	6/27 - 7/1	4
Condon, MT	27.42	1376.12	7/1 - 7/3	
Bigfork, MT	45.48	1421.6	7/2 - 7/6	5
Kalispell, MT	18.09	1439.69	7/6 - 7/7	2

Chapter 17

The All Important Shoe Choice

As I said before, I fretted over every last detail of Kevin's Last Walk. Shoe selection was no exception. I had been a runner for many years, so I was painfully aware of how important this decision would be. Many people thought it would be easy for me to get a shoe sponsor and believe me, I tried. I emailed and wrote to every major shoe company I could think of. At the time, I felt certain that someone would see the benefit in sponsoring us with shoes. They all politely responded with "Thanks, but no thanks" letters.

I also emailed several major sporting goods stores to see if they would like to sponsor us. No luck there, either. In hindsight, maybe it was a good thing. It gave me latitude to use whatever clothing or shoes I wanted.

I still wasn't sure what types of shoes I would need. If the weather was cold, I couldn't walk in a mesh walking or running shoe. I was going to need a leather walking shoe. I also needed to be prepared for snow. I needed hiking boots for those days.

I spent hours at different shoe and sporting goods stores trying on close to everything they had. In the end, I settled on three different types of shoes for everyday walking. I used the Brooks Addiction Walkers, Brooks Beast, and the Asics 2100 series running shoes. I had been running in the Asics shoes for years and I wanted something familiar.

For the most part, I used the Brooks shoes. All three shoe types performed very nicely. The Brooks Addiction Walkers ended up being my favorite for a few reasons. First, they were leather, which kept my feet warm on the cold mornings, and second, they seem to have a thicker sole. It could have been my imagination, but on some of the rougher pavement, it felt like I could feel the rocks through the shoes (on second thought, it wasn't my imagination; I could definitely feel the rocks through my shoes). Again, probably no big deal ordinarily, but this wasn't exactly a stroll through the park.

I also brought along two different types of hiking boots, neither of which saw much action. I did wear the high-top hiking boots one morning when I ended up walking in snow for a few miles.

In all, I had seven pairs of shoes in my bag when we left our home in Gilbert, Arizona. It seemed like that ought to be enough. As it turned out, it was not quite enough; I ordered one more pair of the Addiction Walkers for the last 150 miles. The last thing I needed toward the end was to be walking on worn-out shoes and hurt myself.

Chapter 18

Finding a Housesitter

We live in a great neighborhood here in Gilbert, but I didn't like the idea of leaving the house empty for four months. We would have to hire a landscaper to come in and take care of the yard. This certainly would not be inexpensive, as we have an acre of grass and over 40 trees. We also had a dog named Coal. We would also have to hire someone to come in and feed her and we were afraid she would get very lonely. She never liked it when we were away, even for a few days. Coal was very glad to see us when we returned. Sadly, she passed away just a few months after we returned at the ripe old age of 15.

We decided the best idea was to find someone to housesit for us. We needed to find someone we could trust to take care of the house and the yard and feed Coal. One of Kevin's best friends in high school was Keith.

When Kevin and Keith were in high school, Keith lost his driver's license for a period of time. Kevin would pick up Keith's girlfriend Kendell and take her to Keith's house. Sometimes he would stay there and hang out with them; sometimes he would come back home. Kevin would then give Kendell a ride home. I guess that Keith trusted Kevin. He trusted him to give his girlfriend Kendell a ride home each night. Not many friends are like that.

We decided to ask Keith if he was willing to housesit for us. Keith accepted the offer. I don't know how good a job he did keeping up on the yard while we were gone, but it was in good shape when we got back.

KEVIN'S LAST WALK

Chapter 19

Training

NotMYkid was able to get Endurance Rehab of Scottsdale, Arizona to sponsor us. Their responsibility was to get a 48-year-old, short, pudgy, bald guy ready to walk from Arizona to Montana. Seemed simple enough. Endurance Rehab would set up my training schedule, attending to all my little pains and, of course, the whole nutrition thing.

I spent countless hours working with Nate, Matt, and Melissa over the next ten months. Nate patiently worked on my various aches and pains, the biggest being a pretty good case of plantar fasciitis. Plantar fasciitis is a foot injury that can be very painful and sometimes requires surgery. I considered surgery, but I didn't feel I would have time to heal and be prepared to walk, not to mention the fact that I hate the sight of blood, especially mine.

Nate spent a great deal of time working on my plantar fasciitis. The stretching therapy he did helped, but it was also very painful. When Nate worked on the bottom of my feet, I laid flat on my stomach with my face buried in a pillow so the other patients couldn't hear me groan. I also spent several months wearing a special sock to bed that kept my foot stretched out. These things all helped to some extent, but it was still a big problem for me. The pain that I endured as a result of this was by far the biggest physical problem I had. Anyone who has ever had it knows exactly what I'm talking about.

Matt showed me the strengthening and stretching workout I was to follow, along with the training schedule. Melissa coached me about nutrition. I knew that nutrition and stretching were supposed to be important, but I had never been very diligent in focusing on either one of them. By the end of the walk, I had a very clear understanding of the critical importance of both.

The folks at Endurance Rehab did an incredible job of preparing me for Kevin's Last Walk. As I reflect back on the physical challenges of Kevin's Last Walk, I find it difficult to believe that it was me who did it. If the folks at Endurance Rehab can get me ready for this, they can get anybody ready for anything. I'm very thankful to them for their great support, guidance, and friendship.

I spent roughly ten months training for Kevin's Last Walk and countless hours and miles on the canals and roads near our home. Also, in order to prepare for the mountains, I made many trips up to an area near Mt. Ord.

Several people often accompanied me on these training missions. Bev, as always, accompanied me on her bike on all of the long runs I did. She brought water and snacks along for me. My daughters, Sarah and Cassandra, also accompanied me on many long, hot walks during the summer here in Gilbert. They also made several trips to Mt. Ord with me. I managed to convince my youngest brother, Lark, to help me, as well. My brother lives in Phoenix, so he would meet me in a parking lot halfway between. Most of the trips to Mt. Ord were done very early on a Saturday or Sunday. Lark would have his wife, Terri, drop him off at the meeting point. She'd often look at us like we were just a bit off our rockers. We'd typically meet around 6:00 a.m. In addition, I had to schedule all this training around working full-time and keeping up with all of the other day-to-day tasks that a homeowner has.

One week, while my brother and I were headed up to do some training at Mt. Ord, we saw some people walking along the road. The support van said something about a coast-to-coast walk. I did some research when I got back that night and discovered it was something associated with Walmart. They were going to be in the Walmart parking lot near my home that same weekend.

I had some time, so I stopped by to chat with them. We talked at length about the details of how one goes for a long walk. I told one of the walkers about how I was planning to walk 5 days a week—3 days at 20 miles per day and 2 days at 15 miles per day. She told me that she would avoid 20 mile days at all cost. While I didn't take her advice, at least not initially, I didn't forget about it either. It seems a guy should listen to advice from someone who had already had the experience. I guess my parents have said that many times.

My flawed thinking was that I would need those days off to recover. Maybe it was psychological. Maybe I should call it what I thought it was—scary! The thought of walking 6 or 7 days a week seemed like something very difficult to do, much more difficult than having 2 days a week off. Also, I knew that there were going to be many days that I was going to be speaking and I didn't know how easy it was going to be to try and schedule speaking engagements and walk in the same day. Thinking this hard could cause a guy to get a headache or maybe lose his hair. But then, I had already lost my hair.

All of this training was great, but would it properly prepare me for 90 mile weeks? Would my body start breaking down under the load of so many long weeks with Kevin's ashes on my back? Would I be able to tolerate the pain I might face? What gave me the most hope was that I was doing this for a reason and that with a little help from above, I would be okay.

On Labor Day weekend in 2006, I walked 40 miles in over 3 days. I felt pretty good after this, but I still worried about my body's response to the grind of repetitive 90 mile weeks. There was simply no way to know and no way to test myself.

On Thanksgiving weekend of 2006, I covered 70 miles in over 4 days. These 70 miles included walking at 7,500 feet elevation one day and good sized hills the next. Again, I was tired, but overall I felt pretty good. This was my highest mileage weekend before we left for Kevin's Last Walk.

Chapter 20

The Time to Leave Draws Near

In October of 2006, we finalized the route and schedule for Kevin's Last Walk. NotMYkid began scheduling schools along the way. They also began organizing a launch for us.

We discussed at length the many ways we could launch Kevin's Last Walk. This included leaving from our home, leaving from the high school Kevin attended, or perhaps a store that wanted to sponsor us. For various reasons, we decided to leave from the Gilbert Town Center.

Another detail that we discussed—and also fretted at length about—was how many vehicles to take. If we only took one vehicle, we would save money on gas, but that would leave us vulnerable to delays if that vehicle broke down and could complicate the day-to-day logistics. It would also mean leaving more things behind because of limited space. We talked about getting a trailer to take along. This would give us much more space for all of my little things. We worried that a trailer might be too easy to steal, as it would have to be left at the hotel while we were walking each day. In the end, we settled on two vehicles. I think it was a good decision as we did have a few problems with vehicles breaking down.

It seemed there were a thousand details yet to be resolved. Bev began purchasing large amounts of the items that would be difficult to find on the road. As I looked at the pile getting larger and larger, I wondered if we might have to rent a semi!

I was going through some old files on my computer in the winter of 2007, when I came across the letter I had sent E.J. Montini at the Arizona Republic a few weeks after

Kevin had passed away. It took me back to the days and weeks after Kevin passed away to a time when I struggled mightily with what I could do to make "something very good" happen. I emailed him again to thank him for never writing an article, and I was serious.

If he had written an article about Kevin, I may have decided that I had done my "something very good" and perhaps the walk would have never happened. Kevin's death has also taught me that things happen for a reason, that it's all part of God's grand plan that we often don't understand or like. This time he did answer my email and wrote a very nice article.

Chapter 21

Dreams

We've all had bad dreams at one time or another: the kind of dream that wakes us up with that deep pressure and sadness in the middle of our chest and makes us think, *Boy am I glad that was just a dream.*

I constantly think that maybe this is all a bad dream and I'll wake up any minute. Sometimes I forget that Kevin is gone when something happens and I instinctively think that I should call him and tell him about it. And then I remember that he is gone.

The Christmas after Kevin died, Bev was out shopping when she saw something that she thought she should get for Kevin, forgetting for that moment that he was gone. And then she remembered.

When we're at home, I often think he's going to walk through the door, but he doesn't. The good news is that he's quite often in my dreams, sometimes in funny ways. I once dreamed that Kevin came back and he was upset with me because I was using his razor and wearing his clothes. Of course, I was and maybe that's why I'd had the dream. Kevin and I are the same size and to this day I often wear his clothes. I'm not sure why, but I find it comforting. Maybe it's because it reminds me in a good way that he was here. He was my son and I will never forget.

In most of the dreams I have about Kevin, however, he is never gone and things are the way they used to be, the way I wish so desperately that they still were. I have to admit, I do like these dreams. I went through a time where I had some very interesting dreams about Kevin. It was during the time when I was doing a great deal of training and preparing for Kevin's Last Walk. In the back of my mind, I must have been worried about whether I could make Kevin's Last Walk happen. These dreams involved Kevin leading me in one way or another. In one dream that I remember well, Kevin and I were out in the woods hiking and for some reason we needed to go across a fairly large river. Kevin went across the river first and then he stood on the other side and told me to come on across. I was scared that I would drown. Kevin kept encouraging me and telling me I could make it. Finally, Kevin waded out into the river and grabbed me and helped me across.

He seems to show up in all of our dreams. Kevin's niece told us about a dream she had about Kevin. She said that she and Kevin went ice skating together. I asked her if he was a good skater and she replied, "Yeah, but I was better."

This poem was written the night after another dream about Kevin. I don't know much about what dreams mean, but in this case, I believe there is a message here that I can't ignore.

Dreams

When I sleep I dream of you
Still after all this time
You are here
Some dreams are filled with joy
You are back home
I hug you so tight
Sometimes you never left us
Life is back to before that day
When we all knew only joy
Sometimes you show us
How you skate and play
You make us laugh and smile
How the world was before that day
Some you are leading me
Where I do not know
Across the most difficult
To a place I have never been
In life you often followed
Now your spirit leads us
Big and small
Short and tall
I know you know
What will be
Because when I dream
You are leading me

Chapter 22

Along the Way

The next several pages are the journal I kept while I was walking. I've added footnotes to several of the entries, which are thoughts I've added since completing the journey. Often, the journal was far too short and didn't include all of the day's events and thoughts that I had. It's a lousy excuse, but I was just too tired to think.

I also wore a GPS unit everyday and uploaded the journal and GPS data onto a website so that anyone who wanted to could see where I walked each day, what the elevation change was, or what my heart rate was, along with the journal entries. Unfortunately, to put the charts in every day would make the book too long and probably not add to the story much, so they have been omitted.

Am I Ready?

February 9, 2007

Greetings Everyone!

This has been quite a journey already and I haven't started walking yet. I spoke at Red Mountain High School on Monday. I really appreciate it when students and teachers come up to me after my presentation and thank me for coming in. It makes my day. I still remember when I spoke at a junior high in Chandler. I was walking through the parking lot on my way to my car when two students came up to me and thanked me for coming in and telling them about what happened to Kevin. Very, very cool.

I am physically as ready as I will ever be to get going on Kevin's Last Walk. I think I have put in more miles in the last eleven months preparing than I will be walking to Montana.

Nate, Matt, and Melissa at Endurance Rehab have done a great job of getting this short, pudgy, old, bald redneck ready to go.

Something very good will come from this...

Is This More Important Than a Trailer House Fire?

February 12, 2007

I spoke at Gilbert High School on Friday. They allowed me to tell Kevin's story to the entire school (3,200 students). When I get in front of a group of people and start telling Kevin's story, all the worries and details about Kevin's Last Walk fade away. I am reminded of why I am doing this and how important I believe it is.

I plan to speak at a juvenile detention center on Monday. The first time I ever told Kevin's story was at this same facility a few months after Kevin had passed away; it should be interesting.

We are all doing our last minute preparations and trying to figure out what we are taking and where we can put it. I would liken it to preparing for my first day at a new school or job; a bit anxious indeed.

I need to get my taxes done before I leave.

Something very good will come from this...

Footnote

As the time to leave drew near, I did several interviews with the local media. I remember how neat I thought it was for the media to be covering Kevin's Last Walk this way, and how important I thought it was. One of the stations I did an interview with had several promotional spots about Kevin's Last Walk prior to the news coming on. As the news came on they had breaking news about a trailer house fire in Wickenburg, Arizona. They covered the trailer house fire extensively and didn't run any of the interviews I did with them. Yup, that's right; I got preempted by a trailer house fire in Wickenburg. Such is life.

Godspeed, My Friend

February 17, 2007

Matt at Endurance Rehab has been in charge of my training schedule. Each month he sent me a new schedule. At times I would look at it and say to myself, *Are you kidding me? How am I going to do all of this?* His note for the day of the launch reads: "The Launch: The journey begins! I'd love to hear from you if you think of it. I know you will make an impact in many, many lives along the way. Godspeed, my friend." Thanks again, Matt.

I would also like to thank the guys I work with: Andy, Doug, and Chuck. They have put up with me over the last few months. I recognize it and appreciate it. I *still* don't have those dang taxes done yet.

Something very good will come from this…

Things I Didn't Know

February 24, 2007

Well, I guess I have been launched. Thank you to all who attended. Things went very well today. I even managed to vote.

Yup, that's right, I noticed a sign indicating that I could vote early (not early and often, just early) on the municipal building so I slipped in and voted real quick.

We covered just less than 13 miles. I have not been able to upload my GPS data yet; the motion-based website is down.

There is a certain sense of relief in finally getting started. It's finally time to get this show on the road (literally).

Below is a letter I received from one of my daughter, Cassandra's, friends. I had no idea Kevin's memorial touched him that deeply.

Barry,

I know Cassandra through my wife, Jennifer, who watches her son, Collin. We knew of Kevin through her and could not believe it when we heard he had died of alcohol poisoning.

We went to his memorial and it has changed our lives forever. We watched as a dad and friend talked about his son. You had the difficult task of speaking at your son's memorial. I have to commend you for what you said; it was like I knew Kevin like a little brother, yet I only had seen pictures of him and now heard the stories about him. I was drawn in by what you said about how "something very good will come from this."

I was touched more than you will ever know. I cried a lot that day and thought about how I would handle it if it happened to me because I am a dad and a friend, too.

I didn't listen to you when you spoke of "something very good" and now it's too late to patch things up with my sister, Christy.

Christy was born in August of 1973. She had curly hair like that of Shirley Temple. At the age of two she was diagnosed with diabetes. She was bright, and very smart. Things would just come to her. She was a straight "A" honor roll student, in marching band, played in the orchestra, and was a popular student. So being an average student myself, who barely squeaked by, following her in school was difficult.

As we got older, she married and so did I. She had a daughter, and then two years later, we had our daughter. Years later, there was a family feud and things were getting out of hand. I decided that it would be best to pull my family from my parents, my brothers, and my sisters, and keep to ourselves as it was less stress. No birthdays, holidays, get-togethers, BBQs, reunions, phone calls, nothing whatsoever. In May of 2006, I received a call from

92

my mom: Christy had passed away. I was stunned. She was way too young. I didn't get to say goodbye to my sister. How could I have let this happen? My other sister Jamie called a short time later. We decided to work together on a slide show for Christy's funeral. I think it helped us both deal with this great loss.

I never got to tell Christy how sorry I was for not speaking to her. I will never be able to forgive myself. I am very proud of Christy and she will be forever in my heart. I loved her.

I remember what you had said and I should have listened the first time, and that is the reason I am writing this.

I have since patched things up with my family. We now do things together as a family again. Last year, I helped my dad get his first elk, which meant a lot to me. We have started a business of our own and donate our services to good causes. Life is too short. Don't wait to do something very good. You may not have a chance tomorrow.

Thank you for inspiring me to do something very good.

Clint

Thank you, Clint. "Something very good" is something very good, no matter when it's done.

Still need to ice these legs and get in the shower.

Something very good will come from this...

The Salute and a Mother's Thank You

February 25, 2007

Tomorrow the real fun begins. Steady incline today (1,200-foot elevation change). We finished about a mile from the turnoff to Four Peaks (for you folks keeping score at home). Also, for the record, taxes are signed and sent in.

We had a visit from a nice man by the name of Jim. He and his family saw one of the news articles. They were on their way to Payson, anyway, so they stopped to say hello. Jim and I stood beside the road and had a good visit. Jim did something I will never forget: he handed me a small flag of the United States, shook my hand, and then saluted me.

I don't believe I have ever been saluted before. Thanks, Jim.

One of Kevin's old friends, Nick, stopped out to see us with his family; it was great to see him. I remember when he worked at a local bakery. Kevin would take him to and from work. He would come home with the leftovers that Nick gave him. Yum, yum!

As Sarah said yesterday, if we can save one father, one mother, or one sister from going through what has happened to us, it will all be worth it. Amen, Sister, amen.

My brother, Mac, walked with me today. He came down from Alaska to be here for the launch. Today was my first 20 mile day and it took its toll on both of us.

I always refer to him as my little brother even though he is my younger brother and I am the smallest (okay, the runt) of the boys.

When we dropped Mac off at the hotel, he didn't look very good as he limped into the lobby. I guess maybe he looked about as good as I felt. I am worried he might have hurt himself, but as it goes with most guys, he wasn't the sort to admit it. I am also worried that if he did hurt himself, his wife, Cathy, won't be letting him come to visit me anytime soon.

As we passed by the turnoff to Fountain Hills, which is a suburb of Phoenix, I thought about a letter I received after I spoke at a school there.

> Dear Mr. Adkins,
>
> First and foremost, let me say how sorry I am for the loss of your son, Kevin. I can't imagine what your family has had to endure. The reason for my letter is that I want you to know what an impact

you had on my son recently when you spoke at his high school in Fountain Hills. I believe you spoke on a Thursday or Friday. It wasn't until a few days later that he brought it up first to me in private and then again later with the family at the dinner table. He was very touched by the story of your son. He was very saddened by the broken heart that you are left to deal with.

My son, Joe, is going to be fifteen next month. He is a great kid with a lot to look forward to. This past summer, we found out through his older sister that he was sneaking out in the middle of the night (after we had been long asleep) to drink with his buddies.

I was absolutely stunned. In the few days that it took me to have an alarm system installed, I caught him coming back in the house, very drunk. We knew we had to take drastic measures. We took him to counseling, etc. We told him more than once that kids can die (accidentally) by drinking in excess. But I really don't think he believed us.

I now know in my heart that he has been changed by your visit that day to his health class. I have been getting more "I love yous" and hugs. Every few days, I catch him shaking his head, and when I ask what's going on, he either tells me he can't believe you are going to walk that far, or how sad he is about your tragedy.

Over the Christmas holiday, I had all of our old videos transferred to DVD. The kids had not seen them ever. For the first time, he saw himself as a little boy growing up. The reason I mention this is that he talked about watching the movie you had of Kevin growing up and realized that this could happen to any young man—like himself—who just made a mistake.

We will be praying for you on your journey. Again, thank you for sharing your story.

Something very good will come from this…

Footnote

I learned a short time later that apparently sun block does have a shelf life. Mac had gotten sunburned, but swore he was putting on the sun block I had given him. When I started using the same sun block, I started getting sunburned. Hmm, maybe this sun block is expired? I threw it away and started using the fresh sun block.

Jim and his family kept pretty close tabs on how we were doing all the way. The flag hung on my backpack the entire walk, and I still have it today. It's a very special memory indeed.

Don't Let Me Sleep Too Long

February 26, 2007

Happy birthday, Sarah! I didn't get a cake made for her. I will do that when I return. Today Sarah turns 22. Kevin would have turned 20. They used to share their day with each other.

Here I am out here on the road on Kevin's birthday with his ashes in my backpack. Never in a million years did I think…

This was the first day of good-sized hills. This hill had our full attention by the time Ed and I got to the top. Actually, this hill is nice. Nice to know it's behind me. By the way, when does a hill become a mountain? I am thinking this may qualify for mountain status, but not sure.

The only problem we had today was during naptime. It was only supposed to be a ten minute nap, but *somebody* let me sleep for 20 minutes. We will continue to work on these issues.

We finished right at Sunflower, Arizona (Mile Post 218 on highway 87). I am icing my knees as I write this. Next will be a hot shower and then, that's right, oh yeah, baby, dreamland.

Something very good will come from this…

Ingrown Toenails and Help From Above

February 27, 2007

Another good day of hills and plenty of wind. As Sarah said, Kevin was looking after us today; the wind was at our back all day. He must have known that the old man needed a little push.

My dad and his wife, Helen, stopped out to see us today. We will be staying with them in Payson. My guess is they will be happy to see us come, and even happier to see us go.

Bev is busy trying to get us ready to leave our home. It has been nice coming home, taking a shower in my shower and sleeping in my bed these first few days-now it is on to hotel showers and beds. We really appreciate all of the emails and phone calls we have received; it does help during some of those "hills" I have crossed.

No major owies to report. I operated on an ingrown toenail last night. It appears the operation was a success.

Bev doesn't think I am eating enough. It's tough to drink all of the fluids you need and still get the calories you need. I told her maybe she can get me set up to take fluid through an IV. Just kidding. This would leave more room for food.

Four days and sixty-three miles. We are just short of the turn off to Roosevelt Lake. Tomorrow we hope to make the final assault on Payson. My guess is that we will be between four and five miles outside of town. I am looking forward to my first day off. I will be speaking at Tonto Basin High School.

Something very good will come from this...

Footnote

There would be many days where I believe I got help from above. I truly believe that when I needed it most, the wind was at my back, or someone would stop by to offer words of encouragement to take my mind off of my "owies" of the day. My late mother used to tell me, "God helps those who help themselves." Well, Mom, the Good Lord must have decided we had been helping ourselves.

There would also be many more operations on the ingrown toenails, too many to mention. I usually waited until they were pretty bad before I operated on them, mostly because the operation itself is a tad painful!

Fogging Up the Truck Window
February 28, 2007

The view from the top is always sweeter when you start at the bottom.

Today we walked up the hill between Rye and Payson, Arizona. We ran into snow, wind, and rain. Other than that, it was a nice day. I did discover something very, very, profound that I doubt many know, care to know, or maybe just never thought about. If you have been walking many miles, and you take your shoes off in the truck and put them on the dashboard, they will fog up the window. That's right, you heard it here first.

Sarah and Ed went with me today. Bev stayed at home and worked on getting us ready to leave our home tomorrow for four months. I am going to miss everyone. Cassandra, I am going to miss you and Collin. I miss you already. I am hoping to see our granddaughter, Trinity, this weekend before we get too far away.

Sarah had her first experience driving the big blue Ford. Yee-haw.

Something very good will come from this…

Leaving Home With a Purpose
March 1, 2007

Today we drove away from our home for the final time as we headed out on Kevin's Last Walk. I thought a lot about what lay in front of us. One of the big things that kept me up at night was whether I have what it's going to take to make it all the way to

Montana. I never talked with anyone about it, but what happens if this is a miserable failure? Would it devastate me? I am sure there are many other people who are worried I won't make it, but not a single soul has said it. As the saying goes, "Work like it's all up to me, and pray like it's all up to Him." If it's in God's plans, I will make it. If not, I won't. All of the days and nights spent fretting over what to take and what to leave behind are over. It's time to pack what we think we need and hit the road.

I had several lists going of what to bring. We talked about how many pairs of shoes, what type, how many pairs of socks, how many changes of clothes and what types. What if we have several cold days in a row? How often are we (as in the royal we) going to have time for laundry? If it gets really cold, do I have clothes that are good enough for really cold weather? At one point, when Bev and I had been pouring over the lists, I actually did a dry run of packing the truck and the car. I needed to figure out how much we could bring, given the space we had. We also had to figure out where to put things in the back of the truck so that we could get at them if needed, and—another minor detail—be able to find them when needed.

Bev said, "Well, Dear, maybe we can see if we can get a trucker to pick up the whole house and bring it along. Would that help?" I can safely say that a sense of humor was an absolutely essential part of this.

I guess it's safe to say that Kevin's Last Walk has given me a purpose when I needed it most.

I believe that if we teach children to find the things that bring them joy and purpose in their lives, many of today's problems will disappear. When a person loses their way in life, it's often because they have lost their joy and purpose in life. As always, it starts with the adults setting the example, doing things that they enjoy, and living with purpose.

Where you find that joy and purpose is up to you. I think it's neat to do nice things for others. You can start with simple things like holding the door open for others, or offering to let someone with just a few items go in front of you at the store.

Another neat thing to do is to give anonymous gifts. Sometimes when I buy a cup of coffee at the coffee shop, I will give the clerk a 20 dollar bill and tell them to use it to pay for the next customers that come in.

It's interesting to me that when our children are young, they do things they enjoy doing and they often want to help and contribute. But as they get older, somewhere in the 6th to 8th grade, for some reason, they stop doing those things. I believe it's important to encourage them to continue to do those things that they enjoy and to be kind.

I strongly encourage music, singing, and any physical activities. It doesn't matter how good they are at it. The most important thing is that they enjoy what they are doing. I think it's obvious to all of us when we see someone doing something they truly enjoy.

I recall watching one of the students in Anaconda, Montana entertain everyone on the piano while I got ready to speak. It was very obvious this person enjoyed playing the piano.

I also believe that we should get our youth involved in volunteering. The more our youth are connected with society, the better they understand that they can contribute and make a difference to someone, the better off they are.

As parents, I realize that sometimes this means more work or sacrifice for you, but I believe that it will pay off in the long run. If your child wants to play a musical instrument, find a way to make it happen.

I'm not here to tell you what to do or how to do it or what should bring you joy and purpose. You need to find it yourself. Keep in mind that it's okay if you don't find it right away or if you find new things that bring you joy. Hug your parents, children, and loved ones. Tell them that you love them every day.

I also believe that staying busy is very important. There is an old saying that goes something like this: "Idle hands are the devil's workshop." The busier you are, the less time you have to think about all of your problems, get bored, be depressed, or get in trouble.

I believe it's also very important to find a job where you are doing things that you enjoy and that you have a boss that you like. Seems a bit simple-minded, I know, but it's very true. Most of us, at one time or another, have had a job or a boss that we disliked a great deal (or maybe even hated). Often, when you are in this situation, you don't realize how miserable you are and how miserable you make those around you. It's safe to say that the more you dislike your boss or your job, the more likely you are to "drown your sorrows."

Assume that all jobs pay the same, and select a career and employer based on this. If you are really doing something you love, you will find a way to make ends meet.

If you have a boss you don't like or a job you don't like, you need to find another job. Please understand, I am not saying, "Go out and quit your job tomorrow if you don't like it." I am saying, "If you don't like your job, don't sit around and mope; do something about it. Start looking for another job today."

My daughter, Cassandra's favorite sayings is, "The happiest people don't necessarily have the best of everything; they make the best of whatever comes their way." So very true.

Something very good will come from this…

Two Young Ladies Were Listening and A Ride in a Tow Truck

March 2, 2007

Once a man was walking along a beach. The sun was shining and it was a beautiful day. Off in the distance, he could see a person going back and forth between the surf's edge and the beach, throwing starfish back into the water. As the man approached, he could see that there were hundreds of starfish stranded on the sand as the result of the natural action of the tide.

The man was struck by the apparent futility of the task. There were far too many starfish. Many of them were sure to perish.

101

As he approached, the person continued the task of picking up starfish one by one and throwing them into the surf.

As he came up to the person, he said, "You must be crazy. There are thousands of miles of beach covered with starfish. You can't possibly make a difference." The person looked at the man. He then stooped down and picked up one more starfish and threw it back into the ocean. He turned back to the man and said, "It sure made a difference to that one!"

After I spoke at Tonto Basin, two girls approached the counselor there and admitted they had been drinking on the weekends, but had no idea it was a problem.

If you ever see someone "throwing starfish back into the ocean," maybe it would be a good idea to stop and help him.

On to more serious matters: we have had an ongoing discussion about restroom facilities for Bev and Sarah. So far, they have been able to "hold it" until we get to a facility. Now, I am not a gambling man, but I am guessing this won't last until Montana. If anyone gets an office pool going on the date that they break down, let me know and I will keep you posted.

Things went pretty well today except that the truck broke down. That dang truck. You can plan, prepare, have someone you trust go over the truck from head to toe and, well, it can still break down. Here we are, only 100 miles from town and already, vehicle problems.

We were about 18 miles into the day. I asked Bev to go another two miles up the road and wait there. I came around a sharp turn in the road, and there she was. "Well," I thought, "Either she thinks I can't make it, or she lost track of the mileage." When I got to the truck, I told her I wasn't ready to call it a day. She told me the truck was ready to call it a day because it was leaking oil out of the rear end. I took a look under the rear end and saw oil all over the inside of the tire and the fender. Hmm, maybe this is close enough to 20 miles for today.

Truth be told, we are very lucky that the truck broke down where it did. There was plenty of room to pull over, not too far out of town, and I did get in almost 20 miles. I have always said,

I would rather be lucky than good, and in this case, luck was with us.

Whenever a vehicle breaks down, or I get a flat, I try to put a positive spin on it. If you walk out in your driveway to get in your car and it won't start or you have a flat tire, that is one of the best places for it to happen; much better than out in the middle of nowhere in the middle of the night! So, suffice to say, this day could have been much worse. We are lucky enough to have a backup vehicle.

Bev got in touch with AAA and they sent out a tow truck. We did have to wait quite a while, which gave me plenty of time to worry and fret over how this was going to work. How long would it take to get it fixed, how much would it cost? I was very tired and anxious to get back to Dad's place to get a shower and stretch. We hope to have the truck back by Tuesday.

I just don't want to have to deal with this right now.

I saw a Bald Eagle today (no, I was not looking in the mirror). This is the first Bald Eagle I have seen here in Arizona.

I expected these first two weeks were going to be difficult and they have been that. Some of these hills feel like they go on forever. I try not to look up very much when I am climbing a hill; I just put my head down and go. If we take a break on a hill, I ask Bev, "How much further to the top?" Her standard answer is, "You're almost there."

My thanks to Sarah and Ed. They took turns letting me ride their "rear wheel" all the way up today. It helps a lot to have someone pace you. Thanks, also, to my blushing bride, who is doing a great job of keeping me fed and rested (and who is sitting next to me right now and giving inputs for this journal).

We stopped between Pine and Strawberry, Arizona. Tomorrow we will take on the last big hill for a few weeks. I guess I better eat my Wheaties tomorrow morning. Time to ice, Advil, and shower.

Something very good will come from this...

Sore Knees and Cold

March 3, 2007

Captain Kirk: Scottie, we need warp factor seven.

Scottie: We are at warp factor five now, Captain. If we push her much harder, she's gonna blow!

Captain Kirk: Give me all you can, Scottie.

Well, she didn't blow. That last push up on to the top came close though. This was the toughest day so far. My left knee is starting to really bother me and being the worrier (not warrior) I am, fear of failure is starting to creep into the back of my mind. 120 miles into this and my left knee is very sore. I am sure Bev knows it's bothering me because of all the attention I am paying to it with Tiger Balm and ice. We scouted the route and I knew that the first two weeks would be the most difficult terrain I would face the entire way. Gilbert is at an elevation of approximately 1,300 feet. At one point near the end of the day, we were at approximately 7,500 feet in elevation, with many mountain passes and valleys in between. I would venture to guess that I have climbed over 10,000 feet. Hmm, maybe that had something to do with my knee being sore?

It was a tad chilly today. When I got up on top of the Mogollon rim, it was 28 degrees with a very stiff breeze. I may have to break out the wool stuff tomorrow. There is still quite a bit of snow up on top which makes it feel colder.

We will start tomorrow approximately five miles from Clint's Well.

Something very good will come from this…

Doubt Starts to Creep In

March 4, 2007

Yesterday was tough, today was worse: I have very sore feet and a bum knee, and I still have over 1,200 miles to go. Is this

104

old guy's body going to hold up for another 1,200 miles? I had carefully—or so I thought—scouted the route, but I missed a pretty good sized hill between Clints Well and Flagstaff, Arizona. As luck would have it, this hill was at the end of a 20 mile day. When I crested the hill and saw the car, I was very relieved. I don't want to get in the habit of cutting days short.

I had a little chat with myself on that last hill. The Reader's Digest version of this chat went something like this: "Nice job of scouting, Slick. How many other big hills did you miss? You have done a great job of running your mouth off about walking from Arizona to Montana. You aren't even close to being out of Arizona and you are already feeling whipped."

I did see quite a bit of wildlife today including Elk, Coyote, and Javelina. I saw somewhere between 10 and 15 head of Elk. Bev and Ed saw somewhere between 50 and 60 Elk.

The air today was crisp, clean, and cold with brilliant sunshine in the morning, followed by rain in the afternoon. It kind of makes an old fella want to, well, um, get in the car and take a nap.

The next two days, I will be speaking and working. I am still hoping to get the truck back by Tuesday.

Something very good will come from this…

Footnote

As it turned out, there were additional good sized hills I missed, but none of them got to me the way this one did. Here is the answer to the question, "Were you ever scared you might not make it?" And you can quote me on this, "If I was the sort of feller to admit I was scared, I would, but I am not, so I won't!"

Okay, okay, here you go: "Yup, I was getting scared I might not make it. This was definitely the low point of the journey."

The Penny Drive

March 6, 2007

I have been speaking in the Payson, Arizona area for the last two days. I spoke eight times to a total of 1,100 students. Not bad for a couple of days off. I hope I managed to leave an impression with at least a few of the students.

I would like to thank the kids at Frontier Elementary School in Payson. They did a "penny drive" to raise funds to help with Kevin's Last Walk. They raised 125 dollars in pennies. We are very grateful for their efforts. We had no idea they were doing this. Someday, I hope to find a way to return the favor in a special way.

The principal brought the pennies up and gave them to me as she was introducing me and telling the students how much they had raised. It was a very touching moment that took me by surprise. Well, I guess I can admit that I started crying. I looked over at Bev. No help there; she was crying too. These students found a way to contribute to Kevin's Last Walk. I guess the old saying is true: Where there is a will, there is a way.

Abigail is a counselor in the Payson area. She was responsible for coordinating all the speaking engagements in Payson. She did a great job and put up with my being confused about where I was to go next.

Tomorrow we leave my dad and Helen's place and head for Flagstaff. They have been very gracious hosts and we really appreciate them opening up their home to us. The plan is to speak at Pine Elementary School tomorrow morning at 9:00 a.m. I will then get in as many miles as I can before dark.

The blue Ford is back on the road; both rear seals were replaced. It has a lot of work to do before going back into semi-retirement.

Something very good will come from this…

Footnote

This penny drive was one of the neatest things that happened to us out on the road. These kids raised 12,500 pennies! We had many other times along the way where people would stop and make contributions. These people were not wealthy. In fact, many of them, I would guess, could not afford to contribute. But they wanted to. They wanted to help in any way they could for their own personal reasons. Some would contribute money; others brought us food, water, and always words of encouragement. As my wise better half advised me, "It would not be right to say no, to deny them their joy." Well said, Darlin', well said. I am humbled and thankful for all who contributed.

Trying Not to Think Too Much

March 7, 2007

Things went well today. It was a very nice walk through the cool pines. We had some rain, but very little wind.

We have crossed over the 10% point of this journey; yup, you can put one little green dot at the bottom of your screen on the progress bar. We finished at Mormon Lake today.

I spoke in Pine this morning. They were a great group of kids. Principal Clark was kind enough to adjust his schedule to save us over two hours of driving time.

Something very good will come from this…

Footnote

In the beginning, I paid way too much attention to how far I had gone and how far I had to go. It didn't take me too long to figure out that I shouldn't pay much attention to these details. They will drive you nuts if you let them.

Marital Vows

March 8, 2007

Today, for the first time, Sarah walked all 20 miles with me. Yippee-aye oh ka-yay! Great job. It was a very nice stroll today through big green Ponderosa pines and billowy white clouds overhead. The high today was in the mid 50s and oh yeah, baby, downhill.

I am starting to get my legs back. They were MIA (missing in action) for the last few days.

Bev found a total of 26 cents on the road today and because she was honest and told me about it, I won't dock her pay (after all, she did find it while she was "on the clock"). When I told her about my generous offer, she mentioned that we may need to renegotiate her contract when we get back. She said she agreed to "love, honor, and obey," but doesn't remember anything about supporting a 1,400 mile walk.

Footnote

I was very pleased to feel that my legs were coming back. As it turns out, I would have many more days when my legs would feel like they left me. I'm glad I didn't know then what I know now.

Saying Goodbye to the Ponderosa Pines

March 9, 2007

My legs continue to feel better. We left behind the Lake Mary road today. I have really enjoyed the last two days. There was very little traffic, nice shoulders most of the way, and spectacular scenery. We are now headed north on Highway 89. This highway has been very busy so far. We will be on it until we are north of Salt Lake City. We will be leaving the Ponderosa pines behind tomorrow, and head into the high northern Arizona desert. I am

108

going to miss those trees. Long live the Ponderosa Pine!

We finished just outside of Flagstaff. As of this moment, I plan to take tomorrow off. I plan to spend most of tomorrow off my feet. I will ice my legs, stretch, and do my best to get ready to go again.

Something very good will come from this...

Tall Pines in the Rear View Mirror

March 11, 2007

Today was a long day. I put in almost 22 miles. The morning started out with high winds and uphill roads. In the afternoon, I had plenty of downhill. Sarah's fiancé, Ed, did 18 miles with me today.

The tall pines of northern Arizona are behind us now. It was interesting to see them gradually disappear, being replaced by the short Juniper pine trees. By the end of the day, most of those had disappeared, giving way to mostly grassland.

We had a D.P.S. officer stop by and check on us today; he is the first D.P.S. officer to stop by. He said that he stopped because when you see a vehicle pulled off to the side of the road, and several people standing around out here, that means they are probably broken down. We also had more people stop and ask us if we needed a ride. I think it shows that most folks are anxious to help and that this world isn't all bad.

Things are going well. Tomorrow I have two speaking engagements and I will do my best to fit in 15 miles.

Something very good will come from this...

It's Up to All of Us

March 12, 2007

Today was a short day walking, but a pretty long day overall. I spoke to approximately 600 students this morning, went out and walked 12 miles this afternoon, and then returned for another presentation this evening. I was hoping to get in more than 12 miles, but when the "road manager" calls in the dogs, you better come a runnin'. The grass is slowly disappearing and giving way to a brownish red desert with very little vegetation. In fact, there is not a bush in sight.

I am very glad I was wearing a couple of layers of clothes, because I didn't have time to shower before making my evening presentation. The feedback we are getting is very positive.

One of the many things I have discovered since Kevin passed away is that everyone seems to have a story about how alcohol abuse has impacted their lives. We need to decide what can be done to turn all of these stories into action.

I also now clearly understand the importance of responsibility. We are all role models (some good, some not so good), whether we want to be or not. You never know when your actions may be watched by our youth. Just because *your* children are at home with the babysitter doesn't mean there aren't any children watching you.

We are *all* always responsible for our actions.

It's so very important that our youth understand that even though they are not adults in the eyes of the law, they are still always ultimately responsible for their own actions. Sadly, many times adults in our society refuse to admit when they have done something wrong. I have a great deal of respect for those public figures that own up to their mistakes.

Maybe that is one of the important messages here. When we do something wrong, we need to take responsibility for that mistake and move on. As adults, I believe we should admit to our mistakes and not make any excuses. Admitting ownership for a mistake would set a great example for our youth.

If a young adult is looking for an excuse for why they did something stupid, there will always be one. I have heard lots of them, and most teachers and counselors have heard every one in the book. If you are looking for excuses for your bad behavior, there will always be one. There will always be someone out there whom you can blame for your circumstances, but there is only one person who has absolute power to change your circumstances and that is *you*. You and you alone have complete control of how your life is going to go.

I read an article some time back about alcohol problems with underage drinking and I saw a great quote. The author said, "Kids don't pay much attention to what we say, but they watch closely what we do."

I have become painfully aware of the fact that as a society, we do a lousy job of discouraging our children from drinking. Hollywood has comedies that are based on alcoholics. They make it all sound very funny and harmless, but they don't tell you about the dark side of alcohol. They don't tell you that alcohol kills more than all illegal drugs combined, by far. They don't tell you about the lives it destroys. They don't tell you that the younger you start drinking, the more likely you are to become an alcoholic. They don't tell you that most illegal drugs are tried for the first time under the influence of alcohol. They don't tell you about the billions of dollars it costs each and every one of us every year in medical costs, lost work, and prison expenses. As a nation, 3% of the deaths are a result of alcohol.

Before Kevin died, I didn't understand how big of a problem alcohol is in our country. Since Kevin died, I have heard story after story about how alcohol has destroyed lives. I truly believe that everyone has been impacted by alcohol, whether as a result of their own behavior, or someone close to them that has been negatively impacted by alcohol. Most people don't think about the fact that it only takes once for something terrible and tragic to happen.

In Kevin's case, he is the one who was ultimately responsible for his death. Of course, I understand that many things led up to Kevin's death. I bear some responsibility, as I am his father. There were also adults at this party that knew better.

In the end, though, Kevin and Kevin alone is the only person who could have absolutely, positively prevented it. Kevin paid the ultimate price for one bad decision. I am sure that if he could speak today, he would tell you he made a terrible mistake and that he would give anything to go back to the beginning of that fateful night and change it all.

We all would, Kevin, we all would.

What happened to Kevin happens far too often. When someone passes out, that is the beginning of alcohol poisoning. If someone has been drinking and you can't get them to wake up, get them to a hospital right away.

In Kevin's case, the people at the party chose to put him to bed and come in every now and then and make sure he was lying on his side in case he vomited. I know that for many youth—and probably adults—the idea of taking someone who has passed out to the hospital or calling 911 doesn't sound like much fun. Many young adults have told me they would be afraid to call 911 because, "Everyone might get in trouble."

If you are ever in this situation, think about what happened to Kevin, and think about what the people at that party wish they had done; a decision that will haunt them for the rest of their lives.

If the above sounds "preachy," sorry, but it needed to be said. Well, it's late and as we tell our grandchildren, Collin and Trinity, "Pop Pop needs to go night-night."

Something very good will come from this…

Franklin and a Narrow Bridge

March 13, 2007

I got a late start this morning and we are over an hour north of Flagstaff. The shadows were long before I got off the road today. The red mountains in the distance are coming into focus. This part of Arizona looks like the moon.

Many more people were honking and waving as they went by today. The local paper ran an article that I suspect helped with awareness. One car went by honking with the passenger holding up the newspaper to us.

I also did an interview for Channel Two here in Flagstaff. They told me there is a lady and her daughter walking from California to Wyoming as a memorial to a loved one who died in Iraq; too bad we couldn't all walk together.

We also had several people stop to chat with us. One man by the name of Franklin stopped to see if we needed a ride. Franklin is an older gentleman that seemed to be so surprised to see anyone out walking on this part of the highway. We assured him we were all fine and he told us he would check in with us again.

I had to run across a narrow, long bridge today. There was no room to move over if two cars met where I was, so I would either have to jump or get hit by a car. Either way, I was pretty sure it was going to ruin my whole day and part of my night.

I hope we don't have many more of these narrow bridges along the way. Narrow bridges and roads were a major concern when we were researching the route. The narrow bridges have to be crossed when there is no traffic and, often, it's difficult to see far enough ahead to make sure no cars are coming. One of my biggest concerns from an injury standpoint is twisting my ankle. When I am walking along a road with no shoulder, I often have to move over into the dirt to avoid oncoming traffic that is not moving over. Often, it's not easy to keep an eye on the oncoming car and watch where I am stepping.

Tomorrow is a rest day. I will be working, stretching, and icing. Thursday, we will leave the beautiful pines of Flagstaff and heading to Page and, oh yeah, I will be walking another 20 miles.

Something very good will come from this...

What Are the Odds?

March 15, 2007

"Like a band of gypsies, we go down the highway." For some reason, I always have that Willie Nelson song, "On the Road Again," stuck in my head on moving day. We have officially moved to Page. Moving day is always, shall we say, a process for us. Not only do I have to walk, but also we have to pack everyone up, check out of the hotel, move to the next hotel, and get settled in. I also must admit that I have the most stuff, by far, that has to be moved. In my suitcase are enough clothes to get me through three days of walking.

I usually leave early with either Sarah or Ed to support me and to drive the chase vehicle. Bev and the other person finish packing, check out of the hotel, and then come and join us on the road. Either Sarah or Ed walk with me until we are about an hour from finishing. Then Bev and one other person head to the next hotel to get us checked in.

It's indeed a small world. As Bev and Sarah were waiting for Ed and I to arrive at one of our rest points, two cars pulled up. The individuals in the cars chatted for a while and then they came over to see what Kevin's Last Walk was all about. It turns out that one of the guys lives near our land in Montana.

As for the walking, there was only one hill today. The problem was that the hill was 20 miles long. I finished at mile marker 497 on Highway 89, which is just short of The Gap.

It was a hot day and strong headwinds the last five miles, argh!

I have discovered that I have an intense dislike (not hate) for headwinds. They complicate the walking in several ways. First, it's difficult to regulate body temperature. Second, they cause me to have to work harder, which I am not pleased about. And third, I have the wind howling in my ears for seven or eight hours, which is no big deal for one day.

I have a backpack that is brought out at every stop. We cleverly refer to it as the "black backpack" (maybe because it's black?). This backpack has all of my stretching stuff. I use something we call "the blue thing" (maybe because it's blue?) to stretch my calves. I use it at every stop. I also brought along a rolling pin. Yup, that's right, with all the high tech gadgetry there is out there, I have settled on using a rolling pin on my legs. It works very well and I use it every time I take a break. I know what some of you are thinking-no, the rolling pin I use will never make it back into the kitchen.

I also keep bag balm, sun block, and two spare pairs of socks along with a plastic bag for the gently used socks in the black backpack. For those of you wondering, yes, I am careful to remove the used socks each night.

I also have a large, blue duffel bag that stays with us at all times. I (well, someone does) take it into the hotel each night and back to the truck each morning. This large, blue duffel bag has all of my shoes, various spare shoe inserts, and First Aid stuff.

Every three miles, we have quite the system. Bev gets out the chairs, black backpack, and blue duffel bag. I use the blue thing for my calves, sit down, and run the rolling pin over my legs, and try to eat something. Then, reapply the bag balm to my feet, reapply sun block to my head and hands and hit the road. At the halfway point each day, in addition to the above, I lie down and stretch out on a mat. When I bought that mat, I wasn't real sure that I would use it. When I told Bev about it, she had the same concerns: great, one more thing to pack. But as it has turned out, I use it every day; a wise investment indeed.

Bev is my personal trainer (and of course, wife). She is becoming an expert at stretching me out. She says she can tell how I am feeling by how the stretching goes and the faces I make as she stretches me. Truth be told, often it does hurt, and that is why it's good to have her help me. She stretches me far beyond where I would have gone myself. On a few occasions, I have been tired enough to take a little nap on the mat. But then, *someone* gets out the dang camera and takes pictures of me sleeping. I can hear the camera shutter, but I do my best to ignore it.

Tomorrow I will speak here in Page and then go put in 15 miles. Pop Pop needs to go night-night!

Something very good will come from this…

Footnote
Meeting these people from Montana would turn out to be very interesting. There would be much, much more to this

story. At the time, it seemed like an amazing coincidence, but as I have discovered, things happen for a reason.

One Groovy Chick

March 16, 2007

Another sweaty day in northern Arizona. I think I am officially becoming a redneck, literally. No, really, as in the back of my neck is getting sunburned.

I spoke at Tse'yaato' High School today; great bunch of kids there. It's always great when they come up and thank me and tell me what an impact Kevin's story had on them.

Tomorrow is a rest day. Sunday will be a challenging day. For those of you familiar with the Page, Arizona area, we will be heading up over the steep pass approximately 25 miles outside of Page. The hill is not terribly long, probably about four and half miles, but the road is very narrow and winding. I added a few extra miles today to shorten Sunday's walk, as I may need it after I clear the pass.

I expect Bev to do the journal tomorrow. She usually has something witty to share with us. Bev has done an incredible job keeping this show on the road. She is one groovy chick. Sarah and Ed are doing a great job keeping me company on the road. I had a tough time keeping up with Sarah today.

Something very good will come from this…

What's Said on the Road, Stays on the Road

March 18, 2007

No update from Bev? What's up with that? Just because she spent the whole day trying to get me ready to go again is no excuse. Today went well. I walked for ten miles, and then up over the pass I went. This pass had my full attention from the first time I saw it, at least when I knew I would be walking up over it. It certainly presented a physical challenge, but more importantly, it has no shoulder and is a steep, winding, well-traveled road. Luckily, I had no close calls on this part of the road. Most drivers are not going very fast on this part of the road because of the winding, steep turns and they all gave me plenty of room. I am glad to have that bad boy in the rear view mirror.

The weather continues to be very warm, with highs around 80 degrees.

We had several folks stop by to see us today. I enjoy the company and hearing words of encouragement. As I am walking along, I will often replay them in my mind, reminding myself that there are many people out there pulling for me. I remind myself that I don't want to let them down.

We went out for breakfast yesterday, which is a very unusual event for me. Convincing me to leave the hotel room on a day off is no easy task (just ask Bev and Sarah). One of the waitresses is a student at the high school here in Page. She told me how she really appreciated my speaking at her high school. It's stuff like this that makes it all worthwhile.

I am often asked how I am holding up. Well, for all three of you that read my journal, I am holding up fine. I am still wrestling with a few blisters. This being your own personal trainer is for the birds. Nate, I miss you!

Today, Bev changed my Cytomax flavor to grape, yippee! Cytomax is the drink I am using. I actually drink it all day. I don't drink a lot of plain water as I fill up, and the road manager (Bev) says I have not been getting my 3,700 calories a day, so that is why I drink the Cytomax. I find it keeps me well-hydrated and I get some free calories.

Since today was Sunday, Ed and I had a nice discussion about religion, and what is said on the road stays on the road. Unless it's something Bev said that I think everyone should know about.

Bev will be headed back to Gilbert tomorrow to supervise the birth of her daughter Jennifer's second child. He will be named Kadin Harley James. We will post a few pictures of him. One more grandchild we will have to spoil. The plan is for Bev to rejoin the chase Thursday morning. We will probably be moving to Kanab on Thursday, which is a bit ahead of schedule. I somehow ended up slightly ahead of schedule and I am not sure how. I finished today about 15 miles from Page. I expect to be in Page tomorrow.

Something very good will come from this…

Cut Me, Mick, Cut Me

March 19, 2007

I finished a few miles past Page. The long downhill today was very tough on my heel blisters. I've had more than my share of them on this first part of the journey. Blisters are an interesting beast. You know that there is nothing structurally wrong with you, but as the old saying goes: pain hurts!

I've fussed with them, greased them, changed my socks, changed my shoes, cut holes in my insoles to keep the blisters from touching my shoe, and today, yup, I had to cut them. Most of today was walking downhill into Page from the south, and after about 17 miles, I couldn't take it any more. Several small blisters on my heel had combined into one giant blister that covered most of my heel. I had just one tiny problem: I had nothing sharp to cut the blister open with. I tried several things and ended up cutting them open with a combination of a pair of scissors and some sort of implement that had something that could be loosely described as a "sharp point." It would have been nice to have a bullet to bite on, but I opted not to bring a gun or ammunition. As I tried to cut them open, I thought about the movie *Rocky* when Rocky told his trainer, "Cut me, Mick, cut me."

During my preparation, I worried about the big uphills, but didn't worry about the downhill parts. In this case, the long downhill took a larger toll on me than the uphill of yesterday. Hmm.

We had a nice lady stop and chat for quite a while this

morning. She lives in Bitter Springs and said that the alcohol problems there are very serious and the kids don't seem to understand what can happen.

One of the things I have learned on this walk is how prevalent the problems with alcohol are. Many people tell me that the problems with alcohol in their communities are very serious and the problems are as bad in their community as they are anywhere.

I am soaking my feet right now and I need to get to bed. Maybe tomorrow I should soak my head?

Something very good will come from this...

Footnote

In terms of blisters, this day was the low point of the walk for me. Cutting open my blisters didn't bring me any relief immediately, but the blisters did start to get better after that and eventually disappeared. I think that part of the reason for the blisters was the 20 mile days, which I discontinued after Page. Hmm, seems like someone told me those 20 mile days would catch up with me.

A Police Officer and His Son

March 21, 2007

Much better day yesterday. I passed a sign today that said "Entering Utah." I think that means Arizona is now in the rear view mirror. One state down, three to go. On the surface, this would seem to be a big deal with lots of celebrating. But for me, I still have a long way to go and this was just another sign along the road. My goal is to walk to Kalispell, Montana, not Utah. I didn't get too excited about it; my thoughts are on getting to Kalispell on time, and safely.

Yesterday, a Flagstaff police officer stopped to talk to us. He said his son attended my presentation at Flagstaff High School. His son must have said something to him that really hit home with him because we were roughly 150 miles and several days past Flagstaff. I will never forget the officer's next words, "What you said made an impact on my son. Thank you for doing that."

This officer didn't have to stop, but he did. It's incidents like this that reaffirm my belief that there are many, many good people out there, good people who care. Thank you for stopping.

Oddly enough, my aches and pains disappeared for the rest of the day.

Some seeds you know take root right away; others may take years before we know, still other seeds we may never know what became of them. Still we must plant them.

I will never know how many kids I reach. I do, however, know that when I spoke at that Flagstaff High School, there were roughly 700 students in the audience. You could hear a pin drop in the auditorium as I shared Kevin's story.

Today is a day off for us.

Something very good will come from this...

Hiking the Paria Canyon with Kevin

March 22, 2007

I have decided to try a little experiment with my daily miles. I was warned many months back that 20 mile days would exact a heavy toll on a 48-year-old body. I didn't listen to that advice at the time, but I am listening now. Instead of walking 5 days a week to get 90 miles in, I'll walk 13 miles a day, 7 days a week. This will considerably shorten the distance I go each day and give me more time to stretch, ice, and elevate my legs. Also, this will give me more time to complete my journal. Someone called the road manager and told her that I had not done my journal the other day. She is now going to dock my pay for that day.

While I am on the road, my mind often drifts to memories of Kevin. Today was no exception. As I crossed the Paria River, I thought about the unforgettable hike Kevin, myself, and several boy scouts went on through Paria Canyon. Paria Canyon is a spectacular slot canyon with beautiful red and brown rock in a canyon that narrows to a few feet wide and 200 feet deep.

Kevin was still in junior high at the time. I was worried he might have a tough time hiking the roughly 50 miles down through the canyon. When we made the trip down through Paria Canyon, I thought it would be the longest hike I would ever go on. At the end of the first day, we were all very tired, and some of the other scouts were talking about taking a short cut and getting out the next day. Luckily, cooler heads prevailed and we continued on down through the canyon.

Finding clean water in this canyon was very difficult. Often, we would filter and sanitize the muddy Paria River water. The last night we spent in the canyon was pretty miserable. We had hiked too long and it was dark before we decided to stop. This made finding a good camping spot very difficult. We ended up camping on a sand bar that was covered with tiny bugs that we didn't see until we were all in our sleeping bags. We decided that trying to sleep with bugs all over us wasn't going to work, so we packed up and headed out again. This area was known to have lots of rattlesnakes, so walking along a trail in the dark was tense, to say the least. We eventually found a good place to sleep and made it out to Lee's Ferry and our vehicles the next day. I learned a lot about Kevin that trip. I learned that he could keep up with me if he had to.

I thought a lot about that trip as I crossed the Paria River and the turnoff to the trailhead. Never in a million years when we did the Paria Canyon hike did I think I would be walking on the road to the Paria River.

So many good memories of him. I am glad we had the time we did.

I often wonder how I would have changed things if I had only known...

Something very good will come from this...

Leavitrite Rocks

March 23, 2007

If the weatherman says, "Thirty percent chance of rain with some locally heavy showers," and you end up walking in the rain seventy-five percent of the time, was he correct?

I noticed this morning when I stepped outside that it was warmer than it had been. This could mean only one thing: cloud cover. As we drove out to where Bev was going to drop us off, she kept talking about how neat the clouds looked, and I was thinking, "Yup, those are neat clouds and I am probably going to get rained on today." The first few miles were dry, but it was obvious that there were some big rain clouds on the horizon and after about mile three, the skies parted.

I am prepared for rain with one exception: getting in and out of the truck without getting everything wet.

Wet days are always complicated. How do you take your breaks? Sit outside in the rain? I think not. To get in the truck, I had to take off my rain gear, which seemed like a lot of work for just a few minutes of rest, but if I was changing socks or shoes, I had to in order to keep my feet dry for a little while.

Ed and I ended up not taking a break for the last five or six miles because it was too much trouble to get the rain gear off and get in the truck dry.

The weather today was probably much more typical for this time of year, with a high in the low 50s. It was much more comfortable for walking. We are still in what I would call the "high desert." There are a few Junipers, but mostly scrub brush and rocks. I do have to admit, if I had the time, I would like to do some exploring in this area. The road from Page, Arizona to Kanab, Utah is loaded with spectacular rock formations. Maybe when I grow up, I could study Geology. My interest in studying rock formations is in no way related to the rock collecting that has been going on out here. Bev and Sarah have found a large number of what I call "Leavitrite" rocks. For those of you not familiar with

122

this rock, you "leave it rite" there. The door pockets on the truck are loaded with Leavitrite rocks.

Something very good will come from this…

Deer Herds

March 24, 2007

Good day today. The morning started out rather cool; lots of low clouds, wind and 43 degrees. I kept my jacket on until the last three miles today. I will make it into Kanab tomorrow. I am roughly ten miles from Kanab now. Once I get through Kanab, highway 89 takes a turn to the north and I will follow it most of the way to Salt Lake City, Utah. Kanab reminds me a lot of the Sedona, Arizona area: red rock and cliffs. It's a fairly small town with only one traffic light.

I found two different definitions for the word Kanab. The first is a Piute word meaning "willow." The second is a Native American word for a willow basket used to carry an infant on its mother's back. I guess you can take your pick as to which one is correct.

I saw many dead deer along the highway here. I also saw 30 or 40 head of deer the other day running across the road. I have never seen deer herd together the way they do here.

Something very good will come from this…

No Church Today

March 25, 2007

Welcome to the sprawling metropolis of Kanab. It was kind of neat walking through downtown today. Here's a news flash for everyone: There are still towns that close down on Sunday. Kanab is one of them. Most of the stores are closed, including the largest grocery store in town and there is no Walmart.

The weather was very nice today. I finished just past Kanab.

I will start a gradual climb tomorrow. I know the next town we stay in is at roughly 6,600 feet elevation, so I will do some climbing over the next few days.

Today is Sunday, and we should all be in church listening to the preacher tell us about the Good Word, but I think that when I am out walking in this beautiful world that the Good Lord created, I am as close to Him as I will ever be.

Something very good will come from this…

As for Me and My House

March 26, 2007

Good-sized incline outside of Kanab today. The weather was very nice. Still lots of red sand, Juniper trees, and cliffs with interesting-looking caves. Apparently, southern Utah is not all that flat.

There are a large number of trucks in this area. I believe they are called belly dump trucks because they dump their load from the belly. Kevin used to call these trucks "belly rubber trucks."

There is an old gospel song that has a part that goes, "As for me and my house, we will serve the Lord." Kevin's version of this was, "As for me and the White House, we will serve the Lord."

We have moved up the speaking engagement for Kanab to tomorrow so we can leave a day or two early.

Something very good will come from this…

Are You the Guy Walking to Montana?

March 27, 2007

One of the three people who read my journal has sent me an email to complain that my journal is too short. Well, um, oh yeah?

Today I spoke at Kanab High School. The students had

many questions for me. In fact, for a group of 250 high school students, they asked more questions than any other high school group. As a result of today's presentation, I have been asked if I could speak at the next high school up the road in Orderville, Utah.

While I was walking today, this lady pulled up next to me on the road and asked if I was the guy that was walking to Montana. I told her that I was. She is from the high school in Orderville. We discussed a date and time for me to be there and then she drove off. I guess it's as simple as that.

The weather today was interesting, to say the least. We saw snow, rain, and high winds. I believe the forecast was for gusts of up to 50 mph. I would say we saw some gusts very close to that. The good news is that it was at our back all day.

Tomorrow we move to Panguitch. Each move gets a little smoother (go ahead, hum the Willie Nelson song; I did).

Something very good will come from this...

Footnote

I enjoyed trying to accommodate these impromptu speaking engagements. There were many other times where individuals would try to get me to their local schools and we accommodated all that we could.

He Ain't All That Slick

March 28, 2007

If I was the sort of guy to admit that today was miserable, cold, windy, and rainy, I would. But I'm not, so I won't. I went back and looked at the last three days' data. Approximately 3,400 feet of elevation gain in the last three days. It was kind of sneaky stuff: steady gradual uphill interrupted by brief steep uphill. This might have something to do with my legs being a bit tired today.

There was a pretty good hill at around mile four that my fuel efficiency was rather poor on. It took me a Clif bar, a Larabar,

125

two cheese sticks, and a half a bottle of Cytomax to get to the top. I know the road manager thinks I don't eat enough, but I do eat quite a bit while I am walking. I have become skilled in the art of eating a sandwich and walking.

Today there was snow on the highway when I started, but it quickly melted away. High today was in the low 30s with a pretty good wind at times, which made it hard to get comfortable.

I am starting to see a few Ponderosa Pines again; I kinda dig them.

A few days back, I mentioned that I was going to reduce the distance I walk daily to 13 miles and walk 7 days a week. I am going to stick with this routine for the foreseeable future.

I break up the 13 miles by taking a short break at 4, and 10 miles. This short break is to stretch, refuel, and grease my feet. At seven miles, I take a longer break that includes more stretching, eating, reapplying sun block, and greasing my feet. The longer breaks take up to 40 minutes, and the short breaks are approximately ten minutes.

Tomorrow I will go back to Orderville and speak at their high school and then hit the road again for another 13 miles. It could be another late day.

Something very good will come from this...

Footnote
Bev read this journal entry a few days later and pointed out to me that I am not all that slick at eating and walking; just look at the food stains on my shoes.

Antifreeze

March 29, 2007

I almost had to call it a "snow day" today. "We" decided that I should drive back to Orderville as the roads looked ominous here in Panguitch, and I was the most experienced on slick roads.

126

Yeah, I have experience, but it was 30 years ago. The snow was coming down pretty hard and was sticking to the road on the way out, but as the day warmed up, the snow melted off. The wind switched around and was coming out of the north today (yes, right in my face all day). I wore my beanie all day.

Almost a snow day.

It was a cool day, but I managed to make it with the beanie (and a beanie liner), Under Armour, long sleeved tee shirt, and my jacket (the jacket is just a shell). Each time I started out I was cold, but warmed up after a bit. I don't think it was colder today, but it felt colder because the wind shifted around and was in my face all day. Did I mention the wind was in my face all day?

I guess the honeymoon is over. A new Cytomax flavor was pushed on me without any prior written notice, and not even an apology when I mentioned it. Sadly, the only way I realized it was a new flavor was the color of the bottle had changed to a rust color.

As we were checking the sound and video system at Valley High School, I was chatting with the maintenance guy about the weather in Orderville, which was much nicer than just a few miles up the road in Panguitch. He told me, "It's always that way. When we need anti-freeze for our cars, we use the water from Panguitch."

Things went well there. They gave me a standing ovation. Pretty cool stuff.

Something very good will come from this…

Footnote

This was the only day I saw snow sticking to the road. There would be many more snow days, but none of it would stick to the road.

Pay Attention When You Get in the Shower

March 30, 2007

It was much warmer today with a high in the mid 40s. We did have sunshine after the first four miles, which helped to warm my chilled bones.

I actually finished right at our hotel in Panguitch, which allowed me to give the road manager an extra hour off (with pay).

Most of the hotels we have stayed at have low flow showerheads and water that is not real hot. The same can't be said for this hotel. Plenty of hot water and fire hose pressure. You had better be ready when you hop in this bad boy or you might just get knocked on your rear.

I don't spend a great deal of time dwelling on how far I have come or how far I have to go. It seems a bit daunting to me. I generally only think about getting to the next rest point and praying I can get there. After I rest for a bit, *somehow*, I am ready to go again. Having said all that, I did check today.

I am approximately 490 miles into this journey. This means I have completed approximately one third of the journey. This also means I am less than 1,000 miles from Kalispell. Yup, down to only three digits -very high three digits, but still three digits.

I feel as good today as I did when I started, which is what one should expect. I have learned what the difference is between expected and unexpected pain and how to manage it.

I have had many good days and some not so good (okay, bad) days. On the bad days, I work harder on nutrition and stretching, which I have come to discover are critical to recovering from bad days.

I am still changing things slightly, but only when I see a real need. I think the term is, "If it ain't broke, don't fix it."

Sarah, Ed, and Bev are also figuring out what works and doesn't work for them. They have all done a great job of supporting this effort. When I arrive at each rest point, whoever is supporting that day has everything out and ready. I have become a high maintenance guy. It takes three people full-time to keep me going.

Something very good will come from this…

Are You Grouchy?

March 31, 2007

Another nice recovery day. Weather was close to ideal; started out a bit cool at 22 degrees, but warmed up nicely. You know that the weather is improving when we get to take our breaks outside instead of being crammed in the chase vehicle.

Since I think I should give equal time to the bad days and the good days, I should point out that I have had three good (easy) days in a row.

The scenery is very cool: high mountain valley with ranches in the bottom and rugged, snow-capped mountains on either side. There is also a neat river running next to us all the way.

Apparently, I got under the skin of the road manager (Bev) today. I am not sure what I did, but she growled at me. I think it had to do with what I didn't eat.

A few years ago, Bev had to discipline our granddaughter, Trinity. When she was through, Trinity said, "Are you in a bad mood, or are you just grouchy?" Not sure which it was today.

Trinity lived with us for a period of time. She loved her Uncle Kevin. I had to keep Kevin on a short leash during this time because we discovered that she wouldn't go to sleep until Uncle Kevin came in and gave her a kiss goodnight.

Something very good will come from this…

Uncle Kevin lighting his niece, Trinity's, candles.

1,400 Miles is Just Getting Started

April 1, 2007

Nice day today. I walked down through Circleville Canyon and out into another nice valley with the Sevier River by my side all the way. Traffic in this area is very light with wide shoulders on the road.

Tomorrow I need to "rise and shine" early. I want to get in as many miles as I can before I head back to Panguitch to speak at 1:25 p.m. We plan to move to Richfield on Tuesday. Are you singing the Willie Nelson song yet?

The principal from Payson High School in Arizona stopped by to introduce himself and thank me for speaking at his high school. We did not get a chance to meet when I spoke there in early March.

We also had a local gentleman stop by to see what we were up to. He started telling us about the American Discovery Trail, which passes near where we are. It's a trail that goes from coast to coast and is approximately 5,000 miles long. He told us about a retired couple that walked it all in eight months. They started in February and finished in October. He said he thought they averaged 22 miles a day for eight months. All I can say to that is, "Wow!" I guess I have plenty of room for improvement.

Something very good will come from this…

Six Cents a Pipe

April 2, 2007

Short day on the road today, walking that is. Some elevation gain toward the end of the day, but overall, another fairly easy day. We are now 48 miles north of Panguitch, so the commute is getting a bit long.

I spoke at the high school here today. They were very quiet and respectful.

We did have a bit of an issue with the shake that Bev makes for me. The other morning when she made it, she gave me some to taste and I thought it tasted strange. I didn't give it much more thought, as it was early and I thought maybe I wasn't fully functional yet. When I tasted it again yesterday afternoon, I knew something was different. I asked Bev what she put in it. She rattled off all the good stuff I normally expect, but I knew something wasn't right. She took a taste and started laughing. She had chopped up some onions for a tuna salad in the blender and apparently the smell wasn't out of the blender yet. Thanks, Dear. Mmm, salty coffee, just the way I like it.

When I worked on a fishing boat up in Alaska, we were told to never criticize the cook, hence the comment, "Mmm, salty coffee, just the way I like it."

Speaking of the old days—as I digress—the irrigation systems here remind me of when I worked on a farm up in Montana. I hauled irrigation pipe. We were paid six cents a pipe in the hay fields, and seven cents a pipe in the grain fields. We got one cent more per pipe in grain because we were usually in mud about a foot deep, so it was a bit slow going. If we really busted it, we could make $6.00 an hour.

Something very good will come from this…

No More Onion Shakes

April 3, 2007

We are now staying in Richfield. Richfield is a much larger town than Panguitch or Kanab. There is a Walmart, Checker Auto, a Big-O-Tire, and plenty of traffic lights.

I finished today roughly five miles before the junction with I-70. I should make my way through Richfield sometime on Thursday.

Today I walked down through another canyon that the Sevier River runs through. The Sevier River runs north, and in many places it looks like it runs uphill. I know it's an optical illusion, but it looks that way.

I am pleased to report that the onion taste is gone from my shake. Mmm, good (no really).

The weather has been very nice for the last week. The highs have been in the 60s, which is plenty warm for me.

Something very good will come from this…

Thanks for Not Giving Up on Me, Dad, and the Four a.m. Wakeup Call

April 4, 2007

The first six miles today were the nicest six miles so far. I found a trail that followed along near the highway. The trail goes down through a beautiful canyon with the Sevier River on one side and the high canyon walls on the other side all the way. I saw several (maybe a flock?) of wild turkey.

This trail was a welcome relief from the normal highway walking. It was nice to walk without having cars flying by three feet away—or worse—at seventy miles an hour. Cars flying by just off of my shoulder is something I haven't gotten used to. I can only describe it as uncomfortable. Some of the roads have All Terrain Vehicle trails that run right next to them. If at all possible, I walk on these trails to put a little gap between the cars and me.

The Sevier River has been a good companion for me. I have been walking next to it for probably two weeks. I have watched it grow steadily. Sometimes it flows quietly at a distance; sometimes I enjoy listening to the rushing waters. From where I stopped today, I can't see it or hear it. I am not sure if I will get to walk next to it again.

I thought a lot about Kevin as I walked down through this area. Kevin and I spent a lot of time out in the woods together. Kevin used to love to call me "Old Man" when he was giving me a hard time. When we would go hunting, I would be sure to find a nice big hill to climb. He would eventually get tired and want to take a break. When he asked to take a break, I would turn around and innocently say, "I'm sorry, I didn't realize you were tired. I am the old man!"

Kevin was never a great student, but he did graduate from high school. When Kevin was in third grade, he struggled with his grades. His teacher thought that he was ADD (Attention Deficit Disorder) or ADHD. I took him to the doctor, who did

133

a couple of quick tests. The doctor agreed with the teacher that Kevin needed medication.

When Kevin was still in elementary school, he was okay with going to the nurse's office to take his medication, but when he got to junior high, he didn't want to do this. The doctor prescribed a medication that was time-released. This meant he didn't have to go to the nurse's office every day.

For whatever reason, Kevin did not like taking daily medication. At the beginning of his freshman year in high school, he told me he wanted to stop taking the medication. I told him that his grades would suffer and he would have to work harder. I couldn't blame him for not wanting to take the medication. Maybe he was a little like his old man in this respect. I do not like taking any kind of medicine unless it's absolutely needed.

I worked with the high school counselors to set up classes for him that would allow him to succeed. This included finding teachers that would take an interest in him and communicate with me.

One of the things the counselor encouraged was classes geared toward working outside and with animals. Kevin discovered that he enjoyed working with animals. With a little push from friends and family, he got involved in the Future Farmers of America (FFA). Kevin ended up being involved in the FFA for three years. He raised a pig each of those years. Those pigs were great eating. It did not bother Kevin in the slightest that he was eating the animals he had just raised.

During his senior year in high school, Kevin was like many high school seniors: he had a bad case of senioritis. He was failing his English class in March of his senior year and he needed it for graduation. He was always annoyed when his English teacher would tell him that I had called to check on his progress. Kevin would not so politely ask me to stop calling his English teacher. I assured him that I would stop as soon as his grades were acceptable.

We all arrived early for Kevin's high school graduation to get a seat near him. He tried hard to act like it was no big deal, but he kept looking over at us to see if we were watching him.

I remember how tightly we hugged after the ceremony. As I hugged him he whispered, "Thanks for not giving up on me, Dad."

Kevin and me at his graduation.

It was a huge relief when he finally graduated. My baby had made it through high school. I never worried about his sisters, Sarah and Cassandra, graduating on time, but with Kevin it seemed to be a constant struggle.

For a graduation gift I wrote each of the kids a letter and gave them some cash. I framed the letter and put a few pictures of them in with it. At Kevin's graduation party I set his letter out for everyone to see. Someone asked him if he had read it and he said no. When asked why not, he said, "Because I will probably start crying and I don't want everyone to see me cry."

Below is what I wrote for his graduation gift:

Mr. Adkins,

Well, you are finally here. It has been quite a journey for both of us. I am very proud of you and I am proud to say you are my son!

Many of the lessons that you will carry forward have nothing to do with English and Math. You have learned that with a little hard work and perseverance anything is possible.

I know there have been times when you didn't think I was cutting you much slack or that I didn't trust you, but always remember that I do what I do because I care.

A few of my favorite quotes:

Feed a man a fish, feed him for a day. Teach a man to fish, feed him for a lifetime.

The happiest people don't have the best of everything; they make the best of what they have.

You never fail until you stop trying.

Most people overestimate what they can do in a day and underestimate what they can do in a lifetime.

Don't take yourself too seriously, no one else does.

As you go forward, understand that you shouldn't wait for your life to begin. It already has. Find the things that bring you joy and give you purpose and everything else will work itself out. Know that you are loved and that you have people who care about you.

I love you.

The Dad

After reading this again, I find it interesting that the very thing I mentioned in Kevin's letter about "finding the things that bring you joy and purpose" is the same thing I tell students every time I speak.

Kevin was not sure what he wanted to do for a career. At one time, he was pretty sure he wanted to be a game warden or a forest ranger. These careers seemed to be a good fit for Kevin, as he always liked being outside. He had contacted the Arizona Department of Game and Fish. He planned to start doing some volunteer work for them. I think he was hoping to make some contacts and find work with them.

Kevin worked many odd jobs in high school, including fast food restaurants and movie theaters, but he seemed to enjoy the outdoors more. When he was young, he got a job working a few nights a week at a local calf-roping arena. Sadly, the arena he worked at was sold to make room for a huge shopping center. When I drive down the road that the arena was on—which looks very different now—I think about those days. His job was to keep the calves coming around in the chute. I think even at that young age he knew that he loved the outdoors and wanted to find a way to work with his hands outdoors. He always seemed to be more at ease when he was outside and working with his hands.

I could never see Kevin as an adult sitting in a cubicle working on a computer. I do miss him.

I will make it into Richfield tomorrow and perhaps a little ways past.

Something very good will come from this...

Footnote

Actually, this day was a lot like most days. When I got tired, I reminded myself about why I was doing this. My thoughts eventually turned to Kevin. I often wondered what he was doing now, and hoped that he was looking down and smiling. Is he okay?

Even though, at the time of this writing, it has been several years, I still think about him everyday and miss him very much. Sometimes I wake up around 4:00 a.m. and think about the day he came back to say goodbye, and wish so very desperately that I could see him again, hug him, and never let him go. Often I will whisper, "I love you, Young Man."

Fruit and Water Fire

April 5, 2007

I have made it through Richfield. It was a very nice day today.

As we made our way into Richfield, Sarah and I noticed a fire burning out of control up ahead. I called Bev on the radio to see what was burning. She said, "Fruit and water." Sarah and I looked at each other: Hmm, I didn't think fruit and water burned very well. Maybe it was a stand where they sell fruit and water?

When we arrived at the next break, the mystery was solved. What Bev said was, "I don't know what is burning, I am loading up the fruit and water." Maybe this would make a great cell phone commercial?

They say that walking long distances like this is largely mental. Allowing your mind to drift off and not think about all the miles ahead is difficult. Having said this, I have a bucket of ice water waiting for my feet, not my head.

I find that soaking my feet in ice water is very painful; if you doubt me, try it sometime. I leave my feet in the water as long as I can, take them out for a minute or two, and then back in. I do this as many times as I can handle and it seems to be helping.

Something very good will come from this…

Crazy Easter Drivers

April 6, 2007

Happy Good Friday to everyone, all three of you. I made it to Salina today. I passed several fields blanketed in purple flowers. I crossed over the Sevier River again today. The weather was a bit warm, but I suspect I will see much warmer temperatures before I reach Kalispell.

A local sheriff's deputy stopped by to make sure we were okay; very nice of him. A man on a bike also stopped by to chat. As he rode away, he told us to watch out for those "crazy Easter drivers."

The shoulder on the road today was not very wide, and to make matters worse, this section of the road is very busy.

The road manager has decided the next city we will stay in is Payson, Utah. We will move there next Tuesday. It's a pretty big jump, but we will be almost 50 miles past Richfield by then, so it makes good sense.

The last few days have been farm and ranch land, with houses and small communities along the way. This valley has very high snow-capped mountains on either side. Some of the horses and cows come out to look at me like, *What in the world are you doing?*

I have discovered that horses and cows are curious about humans, especially when they see them walking down a road that they don't normally see humans walking on. Often, they will walk up to the fence and stare at me as I walk by.

Of course there are dogs; oh, those ever present dogs. When Ed, Sarah, or myself hear a dog bark, it draws our immediate and undivided attention. To date, there have been no problems with dogs and I am absolutely thrilled. I have been asked several times if I have some sort of issue with dogs. The answer is no. One of the things that worries me, though, is getting bit by a dog which would cause me to lose time.

Monday and Tuesday will be speaking days. I have been

139

putting in a few extra miles each day, as I don't know how many miles I will get in on the days I am speaking.

Something very good will come from this...

In Season Burritos

April 7, 2007

I found out what that bicyclist meant by "crazy Easter drivers." The road was very busy. The cars filled with people and drivers that were not paying much attention to the road.

I did forget to mention something I heard a few towns back that I thought was rather humorous. Bev stopped in at a restaurant to get some takeout food. They had a burrito on the menu, so Bev decided to order one for me. When she ordered it, they told her they do not make burritos this time of year. Hmm, exactly what time of year are burritos "in season?" I guess from now on, before I order a burrito, I will have to ask if they are "in season."

I have made it to Gunnison. Tomorrow I will get on Highway 28, which will take me to Nephi (and I-15). I will then start weaving my way up toward Salt Lake City.

By the way, does anyone know what the legal limit is for the number of times the road manager can shake her head "no" and put her hands on her hips? Also, how many times in one day is she allowed to say "whatever" to me?

I hope everyone has a great Easter tomorrow - all three of you.

Something very good will come from this...

Endless Pavement

April 8, 2007

Today started out a bit chilly with rain. The rain was off and on all day, but no wind.

140

I am enjoying the nice rolling hills and grassland. I prefer these rolling hills to the flat valley I have just been through. Gentle rolling hills give my feet a little bit of a break.

I also have started paying more attention to the shoulder of the road. Often, there is a very narrow gravel section next to the pavement that is great for walking on. The gravel gives my feet a break from the endless pavement and believe me, my feet need all the help they can get.

Not too many cars on the road today. I am also pleased to report not one "crazy Easter driver."

Not to worry. I'm sure the rain will wake him up.

The next few days will be on the long side as I will be walking and then driving back to speak at the local high schools.

Something very good will come from this…

Almost a "Fog Day"

April 9, 2007

We had fog and 23 degrees to start out the day. Sarah and I only got in ten miles today. It felt like I was cheating. The fog

141

moved in and out for the first six miles, but never heavy enough to call in the road manager.

I spoke at the middle school in Monroe, Utah today to 285 well-behaved students. The principal there said that the students were as quiet as he has ever seen them. We are going to see if we can add a couple more high schools just north of here as a result of some of the contacts we made here.

Something very good will come from this…

Good Luck Getting Me Out of the Hotel

April 10, 2007

Today was another short ten miles. No need for the three of you to get worried that I am slowing down; this was planned. I have been going fourteen miles a day for the last week to make up for these two days.

Today felt like the coldest day so far. The high was in the mid 40s with a brutal head wind. The last three miles were the worst. The gusty wind forced me to shorten my stride, lean forward, and keep my hat pulled low and tight. To give you some idea of how hard it was blowing, my heart rate on the flat is normally 105-110 beats per minute (BPM). Today, on the flat, my heart rate went as high as 135 BPM.

I spoke at Richfield and Cedar Ridge High Schools. In the last two days, I have spoken to over 600 students. Richfield High School was added this morning at about 8:00 a.m. I spoke there at 10:30 a.m.

Interesting story goes along with Richfield High School. The story starts several weeks back when we were out walking between Flagstaff and Page. Bev was waiting patiently along side the road for me when two cars pulled in.

The people got out and talked to each other for some time. Eventually, they came over to ask what Kevin's Last Walk was all about. It turns out, it was a brother and sister by the name of Vick and Vickie (I am sure that was interesting growing up).

142

Vick was headed north to Montana from Mexico. He actually lives out at Ashley Lake near where we will be leaving Kevin's ashes in Montana. Vickie was headed south to Tucson, Arizona. Vick and Vickie had been talking to each other via cell phone, trying to arrange a meeting on this road.

Vickie told us she has a good friend that is a principal at Richfield High School and she thought it would be good for me to speak there. Bev and Vickie exchanged phone numbers, but honestly, I didn't think there would be any more communication, although I wondered, "What are the chances of something like this happening?"

Vickie has been in regular contact with Bev since that day. I had my doubts that I would be speaking at Richfield High School as we were scheduled to leave the area today. Once again, I was wrong. Principal Richard Barton was more than happy to work with us.

Things happen for a reason. In this case, I still don't know what that reason is. I really didn't think I would end up speaking at Richfield High. It was too short notice, I could only do it first thing in the morning, etc. Something made me make that phone call to Richard, a phone call I came very close to not making. I was tired and didn't really feel like talking to anyone. We may never know why I *had* to speak at this high school.

I have had a number of days when I didn't feel much like talking to anyone at the end of the day. Often, I am whipped and just want to get my legs elevated, ice what hurts, and eat.

I am typically not much fun at the end of the day. You can count on one hand the number of times Bev and Sarah have been able to get me back out of the hotel room after I took a hot shower. I know this means more work for them. If they go out to eat, I ask them to bring me back something. Most mornings are not much better. It has become quite the process to get me out the door. Depending on how the day before goes, I might take some Advil or Tylenol when I wake up to take the edge off so I can get to the hot shower. After a hot shower and some Advil, I feel much better and ready to go.

143

One more interesting detail: Bev said that when she was talking to Vickie south of Page, she remembers her saying that nothing happens by accident. If it weren't for Vickie, I would not have been speaking at Richfield High. Hmm.

It's late for me. I need to soak my feet and get to bed.

Something very good will come from this…

Rumors of Homemade Chili

April 11, 2007

Much nicer day today with a high of 50 degrees and more importantly, no wind.

I passed through Nephi, Utah today. In The Book of Mormon, Nephi, the son of Lehi, is a prophet and founder of the Nephite people. He is also the author of First and Second Nephi, the first two books of *The Book of Mormon*. I just thought you all might like to know. One thing I am not clear on: Is the "e" long or short, and is the "i" a long "i," or does it sound like an "e"?

I am not sure why, but it's just now hitting me that I am pretty far along on this journey. I will now start weaving up through the Salt Lake City area, avoiding I-15 at all cost.

Today, Sarah made her special chicken and potatoes—yum, yum. Tomorrow, Bev will be going ahead and scouting some of the route through the Salt Lake City area. There is also a rumor that Bev may make Chili tomorrow. Two big homemade meals in a row, ya gotta dig that.

Something very good will come from this…

The Weatherman Isn't Always Right

April 12, 2007

The weatherman said clouds, wind, rain, and snow showers. We had clouds and a high of 50 degrees. Not a bad day at all.

144

Bev has scouted the route ahead. There will be lots of ducking and weaving to do. Sarah and Ed managed to get me through another day on the road, while Bev did the scouting.

More speaking engagements are being set up for when I get to Montana.

Something very good will come from this...

Dude From Pittsburgh in the Middle of the Road

April 13, 2007

"If you have the ability to help others, you have the responsibility to help others."

The high today was 60 degrees, very nice. Our first break today was in a tiny town. Bev stopped in front of a nice home on Main Street. After a few minutes, a lady came out to chat. She had seen Bev pull up and had already checked out the website. She tried to get us set up to speak at Payson High School, but it looks like it won't work out.

This walk has convinced me that there are many, many good people out there. The woman above is just one example. Most of the time folks stop and ask us if we need a ride, or just to talk about what we are doing and share their personal stories about alcohol.

A man from Pittsburgh pulled up next to me, shut off his car in the middle of the road, and started talking about what I am doing. It always scares me when people stop in the middle of the road to talk. This has happened on many occasions. The last thing I need is for someone to get hurt on this journey. Of course, he had his own story about a near-miss with alcohol.

I was confused about the route today, but the routing committee (Bev, the road manager/my blushing bride) was able to ascertain the correct road that leads me north, just in the nick of time. The routing committee is doing a fine job of finding many little short cuts along the way. I have been asked to mention that the routing committee is chaired by the road manager, chief cook, bottle washer, and complaint department chairwoman. Seems like it should be a high-paying position.

One more quote for the three of you:

> "Our lives begin to end the day we become silent about the things that matter."
>
> Martin Luther King

My little brother (yup, he is one of the three that reads this journal) also sent me the following:

> "But they that wait upon the Lord shall renew their strength; they shall mount up with wings as eagles; they shall run and not be weary; and they shall walk and not faint."
>
> Isaiah 40:31

When it comes to the Good Book, I always have to yield to others to help me understand.

Something very good will come from this…

Footnote

I was often reminded that it would be very dangerous walking along some of these narrow roads. We did in fact have many close calls. For the most part, I walked facing traffic. Most of the close calls came when cars were passing going the same direction I was; I couldn't see them coming and move over. I thought about listening to music while I walked, but I decided that it was safer to be able to hear everything that was going on around me.

For the most part, drivers were very courteous and gave us plenty of room. There were many times they couldn't move over because of oncoming traffic. I got pretty good at judging what I needed to do.

I Hate Walking on Concrete

April 14, 2007

It was another very nice day today walking through several small towns. A tad bit warm, with a high near 70 degrees.

The big issue today was walking on the concrete sidewalks way, way too much. Concrete is much tougher on the feet than asphalt. Those of you that do much running know that running on concrete is very hard on the body. I remember an 18 mile run I went on several years back. It had been raining that day, so we couldn't run along the canal banks like we usually did. We ended up running on sidewalks. I could barely get out of bed the next day. My feet will get some extra attention tonight.

Something very good will come from this...

The Lady in a Wheelchair

April 15, 2007

Another warm day. It was almost 50 degrees when I started this morning.

The feet felt better today. I did my best to avoid concrete. I went through several ice water cycles and two Epsom salt soakings since yesterday. It seems to have helped.

Today I passed by an older lady in a wheelchair. I thought about what Ray said to me all those months ago: "How do you think you will feel about it in ten years if you don't do it?" Kevin's death has reminded me, in a very powerful way, about what we all already know. Life holds no guarantees. Had I waited a few years, that could be me in the wheelchair. I feel very blessed to be physically able to do this.

Something very good will come from this...

Hmm, Guess I Missed This in the Scouting Report

April 16, 2007

This ended up being a rather ugly day. The only thing good I can say about the section of road I walked on today is that it's behind me.

You want me to walk WHERE?

We got back to the hotel and found out there was no water. After three hours of waiting, I decided to go take a first hand look at what the problem was. I walked up front and found the water meter lying in the grass; probably not going to have water for a while.

I don't consider myself real demanding, but it looked to me like I was not going to get a shower anytime soon and it was already past 7:00 p.m.

We decided to move to the next hotel a day early. By the time we got to the next hotel, it was past midnight.

I am only halfway to Montana, and staying on a good schedule is very important. Fatigue can lead to silly injuries and poor judgment, neither of which I can afford at this point.

Something very good will come from this…

How Are You Holding Up?

April 17, 2007

I am pleased to report that we have water at this hotel, and it's even hot.

Yesterday, as we walked, we saw a nice retired man hoeing weeds in front of his house. As Sarah and I walked by, he paused and asked if we were from around here. We, of course, had to tell him what we were doing. His first question was, "How are you holding up?" Well, as the joke goes, maybe it would be easier to list the things that don't hurt. Seriously, I am doing fine. I don't have any owies that would come as a major surprise to anyone.

Something very good will come from this…

Watch Out for the Real Big Trucks

April 18, 2007

I keep a close eye on the weather forecast. The first thing I usually do in the morning is turn on the TV to The Weather Channel to see what I am in for that day. Today, the weatherman called for a very cold snowy day, so the next thing I did this morning was step outside and have a look around. It was a beautiful morning. I laughed, went back in the hotel room, and told Bev, "Well, looks like the weatherman was wrong today!"

As it turns out, he was right and I was wrong. The morning started out a balmy 62 degrees. By the time I finished this afternoon, it was 37 degrees, with a few inches of snow here in the valley.

"Just keep walking. You'll warm up, really."

Today was one of those days when I never got comfortable. The wind, snow, and rain were in my face all day.

Most of the time, I can get comfortable walking and then, as I like to say, "ride the horse" all day. Often, I focus on being as comfortable as possible: removing or putting on more clothes, adjusting my backpack, retying my shoes, etc. Being as comfortable as possible makes for shorter days. Today was not a short day.

I am very pleased to be off of Redwood Road in Salt Lake City. The politically correct way to describe this road is pedestrian challenged. There have been way too many close calls on this road. When I crossed one of the freeway overpasses, I noticed no walk signals or anything. The least they could do is put up a sign that says something like, "Good luck gettin' across and watch out for the real big trucks."

Something very good will come from this...

Are There Really More Than Three People Reading This Journal?

April 19, 2007

Yesterday was miserable; today was very nice. Most of the day, I walked through small towns with nice sidewalks, and when I did move out to the road, the shoulders were wide and the speed limit was 35 mph. Much nicer indeed.

Major developments of the day included my first pastrami sandwich in quite some time. I have been eating turkey and provolone for several weeks and was in desperate need of a change. Also, I got a verbal warning before a new Cytomax flavor was introduced. Not sure what I was drinking, or what the new flavor is for that matter.

We have received some great feedback with the "contact us" button on the website.

Okay, I guess I have to admit I may have not accurately represented how many people read this journal. While I don't know for sure, it looks like there might be a fourth person. Welcome aboard (if you really do exist).

NotMYkid is working hard to add a few more events here in the Salt Lake City area. Also, they are working with the folks in Montana to add several stops there. Please stay tuned to this station for further late-breaking developments.

Something very good will come from this…

Footnote

I drank Cytomax almost every day for four months. After a while, I didn't have the foggiest notion what flavor was in my bottle, but the Cytomax worked very well. I highly recommend it to anyone getting a lot of exercise.

How Hard Can it Be? Just Keep Going North

April 20, 2007

With all of the action-packed changes yesterday, I forgot to mention one other thing: a new bag of baby wipes. Now before all four of you scream, "Information overload, information overload," let me explain. I use a product called Bag Balm on my feet to prevent blisters; I need something to clean the bag balm off of my fingers (tissues just don't cut it). So I use baby wipes; they are, in fact, a beautiful thing.

I also managed to get a haircut today. I know that I looked at my pictures and thought, *Who is that dang hippie, anyway?* Sarah and I were walking along, and on our side of the road there was a barbershop: open and no line. My only complaint was that he didn't do those barbershop razor shaves. I was looking forward to one.

We also had an emergency meeting of the routing committee today. I could see some serious construction ahead and no safe route around it. As usual, the routing committee came through with an alternate route that only added about .4 miles to the trip. I will have to see where I can cut a corner or two to get back that .4 miles.

I know this journal is late, but with good reason. I have already received one complaint. We went to visit my cousins that live here in the Salt Lake City area. It was a very nice dinner with young kids running around. This helped Bev with the whole grandkid-withdrawal issue.

I finished just a few miles from the hotel here in Ogden, Utah and with this late night, I am going to be a big wimp and not start until 8:30 a.m. tomorrow.

Pop Pop needs to go night-night.

Something very good will come from this…

The Inside of a Washing Machine

April 21, 2007

"Sit down, shut up, and start eating!" (Low growling noise).

Anonymous

I guess I was told. I can't believe anyone would talk to a nice boy like me that way.

Great day today: big billowy clouds, blue sky, no wind, the sound of folks mowing their grass, the smell of fresh cut grass, and a fireplace burning in the air. Need I say more?

It has come to my attention that I am past the halfway point in this journey. The only comment I will make is that Kalispell, Montana is still far away. I will keep my hat pulled down low and tight, focus on the road ahead, and worry about where I am at some point in the future.

Probably of more importance is the fact that at this moment, my jacket is having its first look at the inside of a washing machine since leaving home. I know what at least two of you are thinking, "That's disgusting!" C'mon, it wasn't *that* bad!

Something very good will come from this…

Finding a Way to Forgive Myself

April 22, 2007

Light rain most of the day today. The high was in the mid 50s with no wind. Not bad, not bad at all.

I forgot to mention that yesterday I had a close call with a dog. I may have taken the safety off of the pepper spray because the dog came charging out of nowhere and gave the old ticker a jump. When the dog got close, I decided to try option one: act like I was really glad to see him, and it worked.

Yesterday, I took one of my breaks in front of an antique store. While Bev was waiting for me to show up, she decided to

153

check it out. As it turns out, the owner of the store lost her son to drugs and then suicide. She has spoken in several states about what happened to her son. She told Bev that she finds it very therapeutic to tell the story about what happened to her son, hoping something good can come from it.

I don't pretend to be knowledgeable about what parents should do when they lose a child, but I believe that making "something very good" come from the death of your child will help you more than any pill or therapy session.

At my first rest point today, the cashier came out and told Bev about losing her daughter in a drunk driving accident. Her daughter was the drunk driver. She left three kids behind when she died.

It seems everyone has a story about how alcohol has impacted their lives. There has to be something that can be done.

I have been asked many times how I feel about the people who were there the night Kevin died.

Forgive.

Most major religions talk about the importance of forgiving. I know that this was one of the most important messages that Jesus Christ delivered. There is no money in holding a grudge and not forgiving. It can and will destroy you.

When you lose a child, I think that it's critical to forgive anyone who may have played a part in your child's death, even if that person or people have never asked for your forgiveness. I have forgiven those at the party, and of course, I have forgiven Kevin.

Last, and probably most important, is finding a way to forgive myself for letting Kevin die. I have found that forgiving myself is a very difficult thing to do. There *has* to be something I could have done differently.

I have forgiven myself for what happened to Kevin, but I will never forget.

On several occasions, when I speak at high schools, I have been asked if anyone was ever sued over what happened to

Kevin. The answer is no. This is the way I looked at it: Will it bring Kevin back? Will it eliminate my sorrow? No amount of money will ever change the sorrow that I feel. But maybe, just maybe, by my getting out and telling the story about what happened to Kevin, it will change the behavior of someone who hears his story.

Having said all of that, I realize that often the only way to force industries and individuals to change their behavior is through the legal system.

Something very good will come from this...

The Tears Are Always Near

Before that day
They were always at bay
I rarely felt them
They never stayed
I didn't know it
But I knew only joy
Now the tears are always near
I never know when they will show
It doesn't take much
Maybe a touch
Maybe a smell
Maybe a picture
Maybe nothing
I never know when
I know he would never have wanted this
But this I can't help
I need to feel him
I need his smile
I need to hear him laugh
I need him to tell us to cowboy up
The tears are always near now
Someday I will find tears of joy again

155

Dogs, Dashboards, and Black Rubber Straps

April 23, 2007

Busy day today. I spoke at West High School in Salt Lake City and then beat feet up north to get in a few miles. I managed to get in ten miles before the sun called it a day. Toward the end of the day, I had a good head wind and rain. All I would have needed was a washcloth, and I could have scratched washing my face off my list before I got back to the hotel. Maybe I should throw in a washcloth with those baby wipes? Then you could call me "King Multi-tasker."

Channels 4 and 5 here in Salt Lake City showed up at West High School. I saw the news piece on Channel 5.

One of the interesting things about walking along these roads is all the trash you see. We all do our best to pick up all of the nails and screws we see on the road. I always think, *I don't want my wife to run over one of them and get a flat tire.*

I also have come to the conclusion that the black rubber straps that people use to tie things down with are apparently not very reliable. We see several of them every day lying broken in the ditch.

Yesterday, Sarah and I saw something that I can safely say we had never seen before and hopefully won't see again. We were walking north on Highway 38, which is rural and winding, with not much of a shoulder, and light traffic. Over the small hill ahead came this large Recreational Vehicle flying toward us. As the RV got closer, it was obvious they were not going to move over. As it got closer, we could see a medium-sized dog walking back and forth in front of the driver on the dashboard. Sarah and I went ahead and moved off the road for them.

I want to thank those who have been writing in. Your words of encouragement are very much appreciated.

The next speaking engagement scheduled is in Logan, Utah on Thursday. We are trying to add one in Ogden, Utah on the same day. What will be, will be.

Something very good will come from this...

Footnote

I have been asked many times, "What was the most bizarre thing you saw on your journey?" I can safely say that the RV with the dog on the dashboard wins the prize.

A Stroll Down Loose Dog Lane

April 24, 2007

Quote of the day:

"I have the truck keys, your wallet, and the truck.
Ya wanna keep talkin', Slick?"

Anonymous
(But I think most of you can guess who.)

Ed and I got a nice break from the highway today. We found a dirt road short cut.

The weather is improving day by day. I renamed the road we were on today "Loose Dog Lane." There were way too many loose dogs for me. I have found that as long as I stay on the opposite side of the road from the dogs, they don't tend to cross the road—so far anyway.

I am almost back to Highway 91 just north of Logan, Utah.

Something very good will come from this...

A Child Lost Twenty Years Ago

April 25, 2007

We are finally on Highway 91 headed toward Pocatello, Idaho. It took several meetings of the routing committee, hand written directions, and well, let's call it what it was: handholding.

The highway sign says we are 75 miles from Pocatello.

Today at our first stop by a dairy, one of the dairy truck drivers came out to talk to Bev and find out what we were up to. After Bev filled him in, he told her about his five-year-old son that died twenty years earlier and he started tearing up. I have heard that the wound scabs over, but never heals. As he told me, "We should never have to bury our children." Amen, Brother, amen.

Losing a child changes your life. It can also be a defining moment for you. Often, when a parent loses a child, it destroys their life and the lives of those around them. They become mired in self-pity and turn to prescription drugs and/or alcohol to get by.

It's also an opportunity to step forward and try to make a difference in someone else's life. Mothers Against Drunk Driving (MADD) was founded by a woman who lost her 13-year-old daughter to a drunk driver. The show *America's Most Wanted* was started by a man whose son was murdered. I am not here to tell you that I am in league with these folks, because I am not. I am, however, here to tell every parent that has lost a child that it's possible to survive this by focusing on making "something very good" come from the death of your child. Helping others *will* help you with your struggles.

I also ran into some construction today. One of the construction workers asked how far I was walking. I told him about what we were doing. He said, "Well I suppose you do have their attention by walking this far." Well, I suppose he is right.

Tomorrow will be a very busy day. I will do my best to get six or seven miles in before I speak in Logan and then it's back to Ogden, Utah for another speaking engagement.

I have already received a phone call because this journal is not up yet. . . no rest for the wicked.

Something very good will come from this...

Bagpipes, Drums, and a Few Tears

April 26, 2007

The sign says, "Welcome to Idaho." Well, thanks, I am pleased to be here. After 35 days I am *finally* through Utah. I wonder how long you have to be there to be a resident?

I only managed six miles today, but not to worry, I am still slightly ahead of schedule.

I spoke in Logan, Utah and Ben Lomond High School in Ogden today. The total was somewhere around 350 students. My thanks to Lanny and Megan for making this happen on very short notice. I think it went very well. Lanny also had some students play *Amazing Grace* with bagpipes and drums after my talk. Thank you very, very much. I am sure Kevin approved.

A good friend of mine sent me the words to the Garth Brooks song "The Change." If we all do what we can, we can make a difference. Thanks, Val.

Something very good will come from this…

Ring of Honor

April 27, 2007

Evidence of the weather warming up can be found in the exponential increase in Gatorade and Cytomax usage. Bev just went to a local store and bought out their Cytomax supply.

It would appear that I am going to have to retire some shoes soon. I have had three pair of shoes in the starting lineup since I left and they are starting to look a tad worn.

I am not sure at this point what the retirement looks like for these shoes. I have three choices: throw them out (not too likely), leave them with Kevin's ashes, or retire them to the ring of honor in my garage.

I am the first to admit that I have a hard time throwing out clothing and shoes that have been through a lot of battles with me. Rather than tripping over shoes or filling dresser drawers with old raggedy t-shirts, I started my own "ring of honor" in the garage, like they do at professional sports stadiums. Kevin also thought it was a good idea. He hung up a shirt of mine that he was wearing when he wrecked his motorcycle. Kevin was not hurt seriously, just a bloody nose and a few scrapes.

If only this were the worst thing that happened to him.

Very nice article in the Standard Examiner today, except for the picture of the pudgy, bald, short, old dude. That's right, visual proof I have not been underfed on this journey.

Something very good will come from this…

Footnote

As it turns out, I still have all of the shoes I used on the walk. In all likelihood, they will eventually make their way to Montana to be left with Kevin's ashes. I know it sounds strange, but these shoes have been through a lot with me and somehow, I feel attached to them.

Rocky Mountain Oysters and Mountains in the Distance

April 28, 2007

I have started walking at a slightly slower pace (roughly two minutes a mile slower). Being the sharp cookie that I am, after 750 miles, I figured out that if I walk a little slower, my feet don't hurt quite as much. Nothin', but nothin' gets by me.

I finished four miles past the tiny town of Swan Valley, Idaho.

At the 12 mile rest point, there were several cowboys out doing what cowboys do. Bev took quite a few pictures of the cowboys branding the calves. She noticed that often she would see a knife on the calf while they had the calf down. She asked me what the knife was for. Let's just say that I explained to her that those calves wouldn't be making any babies.

160

One of the cowboys was a sheriff's deputy by the name of Ken. He helped set up my next speaking engagement in Preston, Idaho. He invited us down and fed us some cowboy food; very nice of him.

I will be leaving Utah for good tomorrow. The next hotel stop is Pocatello, Idaho.

Something very good will come from this...

Fear Not the Mountains in the Distance

April 29, 2007

Today was very warm with a high in the low 80s. I did have a slight breeze helping me most of the day. I am still in a very large valley with Interstate 15 getting very close. The mountains still have some snow, but not much. No trees nearby, mostly pastures and farmland.

There is a country song that has some words that go something like this: "I hope you never fear those mountains in the distance." I have learned that I don't fear those mountains in the distance, but I do find myself wondering if I am going over those mountains or around them.

It's past my bedtime, and my feet have not received the kind, loving, undivided attention they have come to expect. I guess I better get crackin' if I want to go night-night soon.

Something very good will come from this...

Of Shade Trees and Lemonade

April 30, 2007

Ed and I had what I would call a "close encounter" with a couple of Dobermans with a bit of an attitude today. The dogs appeared to be loose, but they did not come across the road after us. A neighbor down the road said he thinks they have one of those invisible fences. Hmm, not sure if he is correct. How does one quickly determine if there is an invisible fence between you and a couple of dogs with attitude?

Another very warm day here. The road I am on has almost no traffic, which I am diggin'.

Quote of the day: "I have it under control. Don't you worry your pretty little head about it, Dear." The word "Dear" was used in such a tone as to lead one to believe she may not have really meant to say "Dear."

Okay, for the three (or maybe four?) of you that read this journal, the first thing people continue to ask when I talk to them is, "How are you holding up?" Well, here is the update on me (big news here). Easy, you may want to sit down for this breaking news: I am holding up fine. Uh, well, I guess maybe it wasn't a real big story. Everyone that sat down can stand up to read the rest of this. Do you feel like you are in church yet?

The truth is, don't ready the rockin' chair for me just yet, 'cuz I ain't ready. I do, however, occasionally contemplate a big shade tree, a nice comfortable chair, and a tall glass of lemonade when I finish this journey.

Something very good will come from this…

A Belly Full of Clif Bars

May 1, 2007

Way too many loose dogs today. Loose dogs with attitude and wind in my face have a way of wearing me down. I did manage to get in almost 13 miles today. I then took off for Preston High School and 150 students that were very well-behaved. The principal said that he gauges students' attention by how quiet they are. He believes I had their full attention.

I do have one small problem to share here. I am getting just a smidge tired of Clif bars. I just don't know how many more I can eat. To that end, the road manager is out getting a few things that I can supplement the Clif bars with. Please don't get me wrong here; Clif bars are great nutrition, but I have eaten way too many of them on this journey.

Something very good will come from this…

Footnote

In the years that have passed since I completed Kevin's Last Walk, I have not been able to bring myself to eat any more Clif bars. I am sure I will eventually get back to eating them. Even if I never eat another Clif bar, I would venture to guess I have eaten far more than the average Joe.

Thousands of Angels

May 2, 2007

Nice walk today through Pocatello; warmest morning since Gilbert. I started out the morning in only my long sleeve T-shirt.

Not that I have been paying close attention, but the cemetery here in Pocatello is the nicest one I have passed. Pretty profound information to be posted in a journal, huh? It really was nice with many huge shade trees.

We also had a nice couple stop by to visit with us. The lady said they saw us through the window of a restaurant, so she ate quickly and came out to see us. They called a local TV station to try to setup an interview. We shall see what happens.

Below is one of the recent letters I have received:

Today (May 02, 2007) my sister who lives in Pocatello, Idaho gave me a call and told me to rush to my computer. She started rambling, "Check mykid.com." I did, no luck. "Try daycare providers." No luck. "Try notmykid.com," Site coming soon. "Try searching Kevin's Last Walk." As I sat and read to her, we both were crying.

I wish I had the opportunity to highlight you in our community.

With the recent passing of our grandfather, we both believe that things like this need to be presented to youth and teenagers with no hiding or "non-talk" about the facts. We need to be open and honest when our children ask questions. Thank you for your dedication and for the countless hours of walking and teaching.

May God bless you on your journey as you find peace and solace. In times of deep sorrow, frustration, or whatever feelings you may have, remember thousands of angels are walking every step with you.

May you finish the journey safely.

It's letters like this that keep me going.

Something very good will come from this...

Gifts From a Smoke Shop

May 3, 2007

To use an old weatherman's expression for a day when the wind is blowing hard, there were "whitecaps in the bathtub" today. The morning started out at 38 degrees with average winds of 30 mph, which means it felt just a tad chilly.

Sarah said it was cold this morning, and I said, "Yup, with the wind, it does feel cold," to which she replied, "No, Dad, it's cold." Uh, well, I guess I can't argue that one.

Today was as flat and straight as I have seen this entire journey, which got me to thinking about what lurks ahead: the mountains of northern Idaho and Montana, along with two crossings of the Continental Divide.

I found out today that there was an article about the walk in a local newspaper. I discovered this at a small store on the Fort Hall Indian Reservation. The lady there was kind enough to cut the article out for us.

When I was almost off the reservation, a reporter from another paper stopped to chat. The wind was blowing so hard, we had to move behind her car for a windbreak so we could hear. While we were stopped, someone from the Shoshone Bannock

Tribe Smoke Shop brought us out a few gifts: Buffalo jerky and water. Very nice of them.

Next week is shaping up to be very busy, including a community night Monday in Blackfoot, and Thursday in Idaho Falls. I will also be at two different high schools in Blackfoot, Idaho. Bev is also trying to get a second speaking engagement set up on the Fort Hall Reservation next week.

Something very good will come from this...

Brownies and Cold Milk

May 4, 2007

Much nicer day today: no wind. This area of Idaho is very flat. There are many huge shade trees along the road here. As I understand it, they are Black Cottonwood trees. I am not certain of that, but I am certain they are huge (some trunks are six feet in diameter) and beautiful.

This morning, two nice ladies from Wapello School stopped by with brownies and milk for me. Maybe I looked like I needed it? Their names are Toni and Brandy. Thank you very much for bringing me a snack. They were wise enough to know that a feller can't eat brownies without some cold milk. It's tough to beat brownies and cold milk.

I have officially retired three pair of shoes. I used the new ones today and came to the conclusion that those old shoes are toast, history, shot, gone, kaput.

Tomorrow I should make it to Idaho Falls.

Something very good will come from this...

Saving That One Life

Cinco de Mayo, 2007

Another nice day of flat and straight roads with a couple of minor weather issues like 32 degrees, snow, and wind blowing in my face all day. That hot shower felt extraordinarily good today—no check that—it felt fantabulous.

The snow did not stick in the valley floor here, but it did cover the mountains nicely. I made it into Idaho Falls today. The roads in Idaho Falls are not exactly pedestrian-friendly.

I did pass a milestone sometime in the last month that I never could have imagined before Kevin died. Since Kevin's death, I have shared the story about what happened to Kevin with over 10,000 students. The number now is approximately 11,000.

Something very good will come from this...

Footnote

While I don't keep real close track, I have shared Kevin's story with over 45,000 people. The numbers don't mean a lot to me; making "something very good" come from the death of Kevin does.

In October of 2008, I spoke for notMYkid at a high school in the Phoenix area. A couple of weeks later, I received a phone call from Debbie Moak, the founder of NMK. She asked if I had read my email yet that day. I opened my email and read the following:

> I just want to let you know that your presentation at our school just saved one of our student's lives. You came to speak to us just a few weeks ago. We learned that this weekend there was a party and one of the students passed out. Because of what they learned from your story they were scared, but decided to get help for their friend. They put the life of their friend above the chance of them getting in trouble. The student had to be air lifted out and put on a ventilator. If they wouldn't have called for help, he surely would have died. Even though it's unfortunate that the student did drink as much as he did to get to that point, I am glad that his friends realized how serious his condition was. I just wanted to let you know that your story helped save a life!

Chills ran down my spine. I started to cry as I read this email. Here was the hard evidence that the work I do is making a difference.

Go North Young Man

May 6, 2007

Chamber of Commerce kinda day. Big billowy clouds and crisp clear air. Many of the mountains in the area appear to have significant snow left on them. I can see into Wyoming and the Grand Tetons.

I am past Idaho Falls now, weaving my way around Highway 20. It looks like a freeway, but I am not sure. If there is a fourth person reading this, maybe they can tell me?

Breaking news: Please consider this official written notice that there may not be a journal every day this week. I will do my best, but as the schedule stands today, I will be telling Kevin's story ten times between now and Thursday night. These folks here in Idaho know how to keep a feller out of mischief. Oh, and by the way, doing my best to keep moving north.

Something very good will come from this…

Big Dog With an Attitude

May 7, 2007

Today we left the hotel at 8:15 a.m. and returned around 8:15 p.m. I guess I only had a half day today. Four presentations, two TV interviews, three and a half miles of walking, and 120 miles of driving, and oh yeah, that big dog with an attitude on the loose. While I'm no Dr. Doolittle, I think he was making it abundantly clear that I am not on his Christmas card list.

Pop Pop is a sleepy boy.

Something very good will come from this…

Who Says 1,100 High School Students Can't Be Quiet?

May 8, 2007

Another extended day today. I spoke at Fort Hall twice.

I had an interesting discussion with some of the parents there. Many of them were of the opinion that we should go back to the days of prohibition.

Prohibition didn't work then, and it won't work now. I believe that education and awareness are the keys.

I think that many Americans understand that if they choose to drink, they must drink responsibly. I believe the key is to educate our youth about the dangers of alcohol and to set a good example. I also believe that the drinking age should be 21. The notion that dropping the drinking age to 18 will help end the abuse of alcohol holds no water. The only thing it will do is make the problem worse at the high school level. Okay, I will get off my soapbox now.

The crowd at Blackfoot High School was the largest so far. There was somewhere between 1,100 and 1,200 students. I am often warned that the students may not be well-behaved. The principal gives the students a very stern talking to about behavior prior to introducing me. The students at all the schools have been very well-behaved and very respectful. Once again, today, at Blackfoot High School, with 1,100 students in the room, you could hear a pin drop most of the time, except, of course, at the end when the Q&A session started. It's funny how it works. It takes one student to be brave enough to ask a question in front of 1,100 other students and then the floodgates open and I get tons of questions.

It's way, way, way past Mrs. Adkins' little boy's bedtime.

Something very good will come from this…

Yup, I Still Remember

May 11, 2007

I know, I know, I didn't get the journal done last night. No excuses, I just need to suck it up. The past four days have been very hectic; four TV interviews, two newspaper interviews, 10 presentations with 1,400 attendees, walked 40 miles and uh, that's it, a partridge in a pear tree. Which begs the question: what is the partridge doing in the pear tree in the first place?

Yesterday, I told Bev I was going to put on my yellow bandana and she said, "Why, is your hair getting in your eyes?" It's a good thing I had a sense of humor surgically implanted many years ago.

When I spoke at the Idaho Falls Family Intervention Facility a few days ago, one of the ladies said that I didn't look anything like what she expected. She was expecting a big burly mountain man with a beard. Hmm, well, I guess a short, pudgy, bald dude will have to suffice.

That night, they invited us out for dinner, which I usually decline, but I was feeling pretty good, so we decided to accept the offer. At dinner, one of the ladies said something I will never forget: "I doubt you will remember us, but we will never forget you."

How does one forget a remark like that?

A giant conspiracy has surfaced today. A conspiracy that has apparently been in the works for some time now, involving the road manager and three very good friends of mine.

Doug, Bill, and John showed up at the first rest stop to surprise me. As I approached, I could see we had company, which sounded good, but as I got closer I could see that one of them was leaning against the hood of my truck—something one wouldn't expect from a complete stranger. As I got closer, I could see that they were sitting in my chairs. What's up with that? It was my friends Doug, Bill, and John. I have known these guys since, well, I had hair. Doug and John walked 11 miles with me while Bill went into intensive training to become a road manager some day.

We made our way out of the Snake River basin and up into the mountains of northern Idaho. We finished the day at an elevation of 6,300 feet.

Thanks, boys!

Something very good will come from this…

Footnote

I still haven't forgotten about the people at the Family Intervention Facility in Idaho Falls. I will be the first to admit that I don't have a great memory. Names often get away from me, but how can I forget something like this?

My good friend, John, also wrote a letter to his daughter as a result of what happened to Kevin. Below is an excerpt from that letter:

> Dear Chrissy,
>
> First, a reality check. I know you've been to my friend's website and you may wonder why I wanted to support his walk. It was not that I thought you would go out binge drinking, but it does serve as a sobering reminder and may help you or a friend one day.
>
> There were lots of other reasons as well:
>
> To be with old friends.
>
> To support a friend in time of need.
>
> To help clean out my own mental closet and keep things in perspective. Family first, always.
>
> I hope you know how proud your mother and I are of you. There will always be good times, but unfortunately there will always be some bad times as well. Without each you would not know the difference. It's truly the stronger and smarter person that recognizes and learns from their mistakes.
>
> Walking with Barry was not only about him,

but for me as well. Thankfully, I have nothing compared to him for a reason to be walking. You don't have to wait for a crisis to stop and be thankful.

So stop, take a look around, and know there are always things bigger than you. Be humble, be a friend, a sister, a daughter. Be true to your heart.

This is a very bittersweet time for your mother and I. On one hand, we are very proud of the young lady you are becoming, but on the other hand, we lose a bit of the little girl who always depended on us. Please know you are very much loved, and will always be very much in our hearts.

Here's my two cents on relationships: I should know a little being married longer than most. First, never settle for anything but what you consider the best, even when dating. You deserve to be treated with respect and love. Don't try and force things. You will know when things are right.

Well there you have it, all my worldly advice. It's really not that difficult. You can make it happen. You have a great heart, trust it.

Love,

Dad

If nothing else, perhaps after hearing the story about what happened to Kevin, some parents have spent a little more time with their children. I'm good with that.

Pepper in My Pancakes

May 12, 2007

Folks, it doesn't get any better than this. The weather was very nice: big, billowy, white clouds, park-like pine trees, and a big river flowing near the road. I also saw a cow moose standing in the river.

Now, back to the conspiracy issue. It turns out it was more widespread than initially reported. It now includes my daughter, Cassandra. It seems one of the conspirators told her what was going on and she didn't even tell her dear, old dad.

There is a possibility that I will make the Montana-Idaho border tomorrow. I am not real sure of the distances, but we will see.

Since tomorrow is Mother's Day, I thought I should tell a small story about my mom. I was in 6th grade, living in Alaska. Mom and Dad had taken all six of us kids fishing somewhere in the interior of Alaska. It was a very windy morning and we were camped in a sandy area. I was the first kid up that morning. Mom made some pancakes. As I started to eat them, I noticed black specs in them that looked like pepper to me. I turned to mom and asked, "Why did you put pepper in the pancakes?" To which she replied quietly without moving her lips, "That's not pepper, it's sand and you better not say one word to the other kids if you know what's good for you." Well, let's just say I knew what was good for me.

Sadly, my mom died in 2001 after a long battle with Leukemia. My mom always enjoyed making things for her children and grandchildren. She made me a blanket and a jacket, both of which I still have today. She made a quilt for Kevin, which we still have in our living room. It lies on the same brown chair that Kevin sat in when he told me he wanted to move out. I guess she is looking after Kevin now.

I miss them both very much.

Happy Mothers Day, Mom. Also, happy Mothers Day to any mothers reading this. Maybe the fourth person is a mother?

Something very good will come from this...

Let's Hear It

May 13, 2007

The boys (Doug, Bill, and John) paid us a return visit. Bill

172

has always been on the cutting edge of technology. He was the first guy I knew that actually bought a VCR. Doug and John accompanied Sarah and me for six miles. Bev says that she will spend no more time training Bill as a road manager. It might have something to do with his nap schedule. Congratulations, Bill. You are now a certified road manager.

I did not quite make it to Montana today. It was a bit further than I thought. Tomorrow I will walk into Montana and we will also move our base to Ennis, Montana. Go ahead, let me hear you sing, "On the Road Again."

Something very good will come from this…

Yeah Baby, Big Sky Country

May 14, 2007

Idaho in the rear view mirror! Interesting day today, much cooler. The high was in the 50s with a very strong headwind (my personal favorite). This made getting up over the Continental Divide and into Montana a bit more of a challenge.

Even though I know it's symbolic, it does feel good to finally be in Big Sky Country where my son always wanted to live when he grew up.

Something very good will come from this…

When I Close My Eyes

When I close my eyes
I still see you there
Sitting in that chair
I see you beside the road
Truck out of gas
I see you mowing the grass
Using fifth gear
Going way too fast

173

One hand on the wheel
One holding a CD player
I see your smile
I hear your laugh
On that great day
When the hunting was good
Hiking together
Cold and tired
We laughed we talked
We broke bread
We got lost
I see you with your dog
I hear you say, Bye Dad, I love you
It's all right there
Because When I close my eyes
I see it all

Quit Whining and Start Walking

May 15, 2007

It was much warmer today and no headwind. I also had some nice clouds in the afternoon to give me a little bit of shade. I could use it. I managed to get wind and sun burned yesterday. It's always something.

Sarah and I followed along the Madison River today. It's a beautiful river, the kind of river I could spend all day next to. Uh, oh yeah, I guess I did. I can only describe the homes in this area as "high rent." These are the kind of homes that if you have to ask the price, you probably can't afford it.

I am sliding ahead of schedule just a little bit. Sarah and the road manager think it would be neat if we finish walking one day at the hotel. Which is great, except it means more miles and as the road manager said, "It's only .7 miles extra a day. What's the big deal?" Uh, nothing, Dear, just park the chase vehicle where I get to collapse—uh, I mean, stop.

Also, I wanted to thank the significant others (Nancy, Joy, and Judy) of the boys for giving them a "kitchen pass" for Mother's Day weekend. Or was this their gift to you? Either way, I hope you had a happy Mother's Day.

Something very good will come from this…

Stop Growling at Pop Pop

May 16, 2007

Today was not a particularly exciting walk. There, I said it. I descended into a wide open valley, flat as a pancake with grass for miles on both sides. I can see beautiful mountains in the distance.

We did have a few folks stop to chat. One lady wanted to get a picture of me. I hope I didn't mess up the camera. Like many other folks, she stopped in the middle of the road and started talking to me. It always scares me, but all is well that ends well.

There are still a number (and I do mean quite a few) of stops that we are trying to get firmed up in Montana. As usual, when I say we, I mean the royal "we." I know there are several people working hard to make it all happen.

Bev did growl at me several times today. She should listen to the advice of our granddaughter, Trinity, who told her, "Stop growling at Pop Pop. It could become a habit." I couldn't have said it better. By the way, Bev keeps saying she is going to defend herself and write a rebuttal to all of these things. Uh, well, I'm quaking in my boots. To be fair (for once) I have taken one or two things out of context, or perhaps, maybe—possibly—had a tiny, tiny case of selective memory.

Something very good will come from this…

175

Say it Ain't So

May 17, 2007

We have arrived in Ennis, Montana. There is a barbershop right on Main Street so I decided to stop in and have them clean up this old hippie.

The scenery was much nicer today with streams and trees nearby. The high today felt very warm at 80 degrees. I am going to have a problem when we return to Phoenix, Arizona in July.

Tomorrow will be a day off from walking. It will be my first day off in 56 days. We are all looking forward to it. I can assure all three of you that I am absolutely positive I will sleep in until at least 6:00 a.m. Bev doesn't think I will make it that late. I will be very, very, quiet when I wake up, and if I am not, well, we will always think I should have been.

Sarah shared some shocking, absolutely stunning news with me today. She thinks more people watch *Grey's Anatomy* than read this journal. Huh? You mean there are more than three people that watch *Grey's Anatomy*?

Something very good will come from this...

Nice Goin', Slick

May 18, 2007

Technically, I slept until 7:15 this morning. I did have one minor noise disaster prior to that. I might have forgotten to turn off the alarm clock on my phone, so I guess you know what happened at 5:30 this morning...oops.

I did my best to rest my legs and stay out of Bev's way all day.

I will not be walking for a few days next week. I have scheduled a trip to Kalispell and Butte, Montana to speak several times.

The weather forecast is for much cooler weather in the next few days. Welcome to Montana.

Something very good will come from this...

Profound Words

May 19, 2007

Nice climb today (800 feet elevation gain) that was missed somehow in the scouting report. I hear that the fishing in this area is as good as it gets in the continental United States. I say continental because from my experience, the fishing in Alaska is the best there is.

I had a steady tail wind today. Toward the end of the day, it started pouring down rain. I actually ran the last quarter of a mile because it looked like hail was coming. A truck pulled over in the rainstorm and asked if I needed a ride; very nice of them.

"A wife and steady employment have ruined many a good duck hunter." I saw this on the wall of a restaurant in Ennis. I thought it was pretty profound.

Something very good will come from this...

Now I Have to be Entertaining?

May 20, 2007

Nice rolling hills, lots of clouds, no rain, and pleasant temperatures. I have lived in Arizona since 1979. As a long time resident, I have come to enjoy cloudy days.

Sarah and Bev got as close as they probably ever will to a wild antelope today. It seems that the antelope around here won't jump a fence. They always go under it. I am not sure if that is true of all antelope? So these two antelope got separated from the rest of the herd that crossed the road. I watched these two antelope run along the road, going back and forth for two miles, trying to find a way through the fence. I radioed Bev and Sarah and told them that there were two antelope headed their way. Finally, when we got close, one went under the fence and the other one ran right in front of the chase vehicle. I have seen hundreds of antelope through this area. There may be more antelope than cattle around here.

By the way, Bev says she is working on a rebuttal. So I need to lie low, be on my best behavior, and hope she forgets. Oh yeah, I forgot, I've been told that most women never forget. Hmm, maybe I need to move to plan B (as soon as I come up with it, that is).

I may have recruited a fifth person to read this journal. It's my friend, Ram. Only problem is, he told me I should try to make it interesting, not just a report on how far I walked each day. I will see what I can do to provide some good entertainment. I realize that a man of his stature is not easily entertained, but I will do my best.

Something very good will come from this...

Lewis and Clark

May 21, 2007

Top four ways you know you are in Montana:

Yesterday the high was 80 degrees; tomorrow there is snow in the forecast.

Old pickup, three guys in the front wearing cowboy hats and a dog in the back.

Dude, it's green.

The antelope and cattle outnumber the people.

By the way, if there are three guys in a pickup wearing cowboy hats, which one is the real cowboy? The one in the middle is the real cowboy 'cuz he don't hafta drive, and he don't hafta git out and git the gate.

Today was much cooler. I had rain and hail the last two hours. The air was crisp and clean. I have dropped down to 4,100 feet in elevation. Most of the road today was very narrow with no shoulders, which was kind of scary, but the drivers were all very good. They all moved over or, if traffic was coming from the other way, they would slow down and then move over.

I crossed over the Jefferson River today. It also kept me company most of the day.

Tomorrow, Bev and I head for Kalispell for two days, then back to Butte for one day on Friday. I have several speaking engagements and a few interviews.

Something very good will come from this…

Footnote

A good friend of mine gave me the book, *Undaunted Courage,* which chronicled the journey of Lewis and Clark. They traveled through this area. Inside the book cover, my friend wrote, "I hope your journey has as much impact on people as this one did."

Thanks, Scott.

Message From the Complaint Department V.P.

May 23, 2007

What is this world coming to? I know, there are certainties like death, taxes, and certain people doing their daily journals that one hopes they can count on.

We had dinner at my uncle's house last night. It was very late when I remembered I hadn't done the journal. Actually, I was reminded by the vice president of the complaint department.

My uncle is very skilled in the art of storytelling, taking things out of context, and perhaps exaggerating things just a smidge. I sure hope I can be as good as he is someday.

Today, I did three radio, one TV, and two newspaper interviews. I also spoke at a Polson High School community night. I will be at Bigfork Middle School at 8:00 in the morning so that means I best get some shuteye.

Something very good will come from this…

Thank You for Your Time, Effort, Courage, and Passion

May 24, 2007

I spoke today at Bigfork Middle School and Swan River Elementary School. My cousin, Shawn, has a daughter, Emily, who attends Bigfork Middle School. Emily introduced me at Bigfork Middle School. You did a great job, Emily. Thanks. Between the two schools, I spoke to somewhere between 180 and 200 students.

Bev and I have arrived in Butte, Montana. Tomorrow I will speak at two more schools, and then we will head back to Three Forks, Montana where Sarah and Ed are anxiously waiting to get back on the road.

I have found that the principals of the schools I have spoken at have all been very caring and want what is best for their students and that includes the three principals I met on this trip to Kalispell.

Below is a letter I received from one of the principals.

> Dear Barry,
>
> As principal of Swan River School, I am honored to provide feedback regarding your presentation to our fifth, sixth and seventh grade students as well as to parents and our teachers on May 24, 2007. I cannot express in words how pleased I am about your passion, courage, love, and honor for your son Kevin. Turning this tragic event into a positive learning experience for our youth, parents, and staff has left a lasting impression with us all.
>
> The issue of alcoholism is one that every child, teenager, and adult faces during our wonderful lifetime. Although our young children think that they know everything, they need many tools when facing peer pressure, relationships, and dealing with difficult situations. This presentation has made all of us at Swan River School more aware about the

180

dangers of alcoholism. It has assisted us with our guidance presentations, our health classes, and assists us with our school rules.

Swan River School praises you, your wife, and family. Many of our students, as well as myself, are interested in joining you for your last 3 miles of your journey in Kalispell on July 1, 2007.

Thank you again for your time, effort, courage, and passion to keep your son's life alive and meaningful for all of us. We will keep Kevin and your family in our thoughts and prayers as you continue to share this important message and continue to live your lives without this loved one. As I stated at the end of the presentation, "I know that Kevin is looking down at you and your family with a smile." Your love for him is strong and has made a lasting impact on all of us here in Bigfork, Montana. You're amazing! Thank you!

Sincerely,

Mr. Loyda

Something very good will come from this...

Just One More Hug

May 25, 2007

Bev and I have arrived back in Three Forks. On the way over to Kalispell, we ran into fresh snow on the Continental Divide. No snow on the way back.

I spoke at two schools in Butte today. At the first school, the students had to sit on the gym floor for 45 minutes to listen to me. One of the teachers told me afterwards that the students were the quietest she had ever seen.

I was asked what I would say to Kevin today if I could say something to him. I told them I would say, "I miss you very much."

Something very good will come from this...

Footnote

If I saw Kevin today, I don't know that I would be able to speak. There are no words that would accurately convey how I would feel.

I do know that I would hug him tight and never let go. Just one more hug.

It's a Good Thing That Truck Driver Couldn't Read My Thoughts

May 26, 2007

It was good to get back on the road. I had a nice chat with a gentleman by the name of Jay. He is riding his bike from southern Colorado to Jasper, Alberta. We talked for a while about the road. He said that taking a trip like this changes your perspective of time and distance.

Amen, Brother.

The weather was very nice today. Tomorrow I might take a slight detour on a gravel road that will get me off of the main highway for 18 miles. It won't save any miles, and it does have a few hills, but it does get me off of this stretch of road that has no shoulders and cars flying by at 75 mph.

Having said that, I had the closest call so far today with a vehicle—actually a big truck passing someone going the same direction as me. I think his mirror went over my head. I guess there are advantages to being short.

Something very good will come from this...

Press On

May 27, 2007

Sarah and Ed have decided to return to Arizona. The

decision to come on this walk was theirs and the decision to return to Arizona was also theirs. I really do appreciate all they have done for us.

I want to reassure everyone that I will press on to Kalispell. It's going to take an act of God to stop me at this point.

I crossed the mighty Missouri River today. The bridge was very narrow. I think it scared Bev more than it scared me. The radios from Mobile Phone sure came in handy. Bev was coaching me all the way, letting me know what was coming. Of course she has accused me of ignoring her warnings and going anyway. I don't know why she makes these kinds of accusations. I guess she will have to challenge the call and let the replay booth have a look at it.

Below is a poem I wrote last night. The idea for this poem came after I watched *Forrest Gump*. His wife, Jenny, was dying and she told him that she wished she could have been with him through all the years. He told her that she was.

> I wish I could have been there with you
> When you left on that bright warm day
> To warm you when the wind and rain froze you
> Every time you told the story about what happened
> to me
> To see those kids who thanked you
> To see your face when you met those people
> When your body ached
> When your feet were tired and sore
> When you felt you couldn't go any more
> When you found out who your friends are
> When you crossed that high mountain pass
> To the land I now call mine
> Where I will be until the end of time
>
> You were, my Son, you were

Something very good will come from this...

183

Footnote

Kevin's ashes were in my backpack the entire way. I kept the backpack near at all times. I brought the backpack into the hotel every night. I didn't want Kevin to be far away.

I spent many nights close to Kevin as he grew up. When Kevin was very young, he swallowed two pennies. He was having trouble passing them, so the doctor asked me to sleep in his bed with him one night to keep him on his side so that perhaps he could pass them. Unfortunately, he never passed them and they had to be removed surgically. I still have those pennies today.

Those Letters Do Help

May 29, 2007

Yesterday was a fairly long day, thus the lack of an official entry in the journal.

But I did think about it and here were my thoughts: If any of you ever do much running or working out, you know that some days when you get on the road, you can feel that your legs are MIA (Missing in Action) but you still grind it out. Well, that is the best way to describe yesterday: grinding it out. To make matters worse, the weather took a decidedly nasty turn midmorning: strong head winds with rain, a gnarly combination.

Today I spoke at Dillon and Butte Central High School. Both of these schools are in Montana.

I continue to get great feedback. Below are a couple excerpts from the notes we have received:.

> Thank you a million times over for taking the time to speak to our kids. As a parent we can warn our children of the dangers of alcohol and drugs, but the impact is not nearly the same as someone with first hand experience of the serious consequences.
>
> I know God has a plan for all of us. We are here to learn and share our experiences with others.

I truly believe you are doing exactly what God had planned for you and your family. Kevin is okay and so proud you are sharing his message. Something good has come from this, something great. Thank you again for caring about our children.

It's this sort of feedback that keeps me going on days like yesterday.

Something very good will come from this...

Footnote

Indeed, I did have many days where I had to grind it out. On one of those days, I wrote the following poem.

I Do Not Know

How do I go?
I do not know
Each day I wake
Strap on the pack
Lace up the shoes
How could it be me?
Going all these miles
On this old horse
Somewhere within
The battle won again
I step onto the road
Riding the horse
Until the shadows are long
Warm sunny days
Bone chilling cold
Somehow I still go
With help from above
Never alone
I feel the push
That carries me each day

185

A Lucky Flat Tire

May 30, 2007

Very busy day. I set a personal record for the most cities I have spoken in during a single day. I was in four cities and reached 600 students. I hope I never break this record.

I also did an interview with one of the local TV stations at a festival here in Helena. After the interview, the reporter wanted to follow me around for a while. I told him I wanted to get a bottle of water. As we were walking through the crowd, I found a young lady (5th grade) that had a bottle of water. I asked her where she got it and to our surprise, she turned around and said, "I will only tell you if you put me on TV!" She made the reporter get quite a bit of tape of her, all the while giving him a hard time about whether he would actually put her on TV. She did eventually show me where I could get the water.

We also got what I would call a fortuitous flat tire. We were lucky enough to get this flat tire in town and at a gas station, which was a good thing because the spare was rather flat. A passerby, seeing we had all of the luggage out of the car, stopped and asked if we needed help. I told him we were okay. As he left, he pointed back up the street to a tire repair shop. So, another dull and uneventful day.

Something very good will come from this...

The Most I Can Hope For

May 31, 2007

Company on the road today. Lorelle and Tracy came out and walked with me. They coordinated the activities here in Helena. I hope they enjoyed the walk. I also had a visitor from the local NBC affiliate. Brian interviewed me last night and came out to get "more tape." He told me that he did put that young lady on TV. I sure am glad because I wouldn't want her hunting me down.

I would also like to mention—and since this is my journal, I think I will—the great job that Dan did getting me in to visit with the students in the Butte area: seven schools, five cities in three days. Great job, Dan!

I was asked today to provide a quote to be used in promotional material and I thought it worthwhile to share with the four of you: "When you lose a child, the most you can hope for is to make 'something very good' come from the death of your child and that is what I am doing."

Something very good will come from this...

Another Reader?

June 1, 2007

Okay, I believe I have gotten to the bottom of one of life's great mysteries (well maybe I got to the bottom of this mystery a while back). I did do a journal entry last night. It's below the entry from the night before. Here is the deal: It appears that the server that this journal resides on is on Eastern Daylight Time so if I put in a journal entry after 10:00 p.m., the date moves to the next day, and I need to manually change it back. There is just one tiny problem with this. When I do a journal entry after 10:00 at night, I am usually just a smidge tired and well, I miss it. Then, when I add a journal entry the next day on time, it appends it to the bottom of the journal from the night before which confuses me and the three people who read it.

Several people stopped to chat. They were all very nice and supportive of our effort. Lorelle and Pam walked for a few miles with me today. Pam claims to be a fifth reader of this journal. I don't know. I am a tad suspicious that maybe she is really the secret fourth reader. I will continue to investigate this and when I ascertain the facts regarding this issue, I will provide a complete and unbiased report. Stay tuned.

Something very good will come from this...

Huckleberry Soda and an Apple

June 3, 2007

Yesterday was a much needed day of rest.

Today I started the climb up to MacDonald Pass, which is just outside of Helena, Montana. It will be the second and final crossing of the Continental Divide. I finished the day at 4,500 feet elevation. MacDonald Pass is seven miles ahead at 6,300 feet. It should provide a good challenge.

More people stopped by to chat. One couple came out from their house and brought me an apple and a bottle of huckleberry soda. We chatted for quite a while. They had lost their son at the age of 19 in a car accident many years ago.

A bicyclist stopped by that had lost her dad to a drunk driver many years ago. As I have said many times before, it seems everyone has a story.

The next two days are filled with speaking engagements and interviews, so I will not return to the road until Wednesday.

Something very good will come from this...

Free Food

June 4, 2007

Very full day today. I spoke to 1,000 students and adults. There were close to 400 at a community event in Missoula, Montana. This was the largest community event so far. Great job, Jori!

I also had a surprising conversation with a young lady at the community event. She claims to be a sixth person who is reading my journal. Well, I guess we will see what the tribunal ascertains regarding this issue. If it's found that there are indeed six people reading this journal, this will mean that we have doubled the number of people that read this journal in just three months. At this rate, we will be competing with *Grey's Anatomy* in, uh, well, as soon as they go off the air and all the people that watch it are too old to work the remote control.

This is as witty as I can be at this hour of the day. It's entirely too late for a dude like me.

Something very good will come from this...

Footnote

I have found that the best way to get a good turnout at a community event is to offer free food. I have seen this work many times.

The Final Mountain Pass

June 6, 2007

Very physically challenging day; my cousin Patti and I went up over MacDonald Pass with headwinds, snow, and rain all day. Some might describe it as a miserable day. I would describe it as a day when Mother Nature had our full attention. This may not have been the most obnoxious day on the road, but it's in the top five so far. Patti picked a fine day to walk with her cousin.

Crossing the Continental Divide with my cousin Patti.

As we made our way over the summit, I once again reminded myself of why I was doing this. I thought about my son; a young man whose life was cut short because of one bad decision, a decision that will probably haunt me the rest of my life.

I often thought about this final mountain pass as I made my way through Arizona, Utah, and Idaho. Would I have the gas left to get over it? Would this final mountain pass put me over the pain threshold?

This was my second and final crossing of the Continental Divide. After crossing MacDonald pass and descending several miles down the other side, I now realize there isn't much standing between me and Kalispell.

We had a good discussion today, but as usual, what is said on the road stays on the road. Unless, of course, I think I can use it in the journal.

We also had a good discussion at the community night last night. I believe it's important for everyone to remember that the "silent majority" is going to have to step up to make a change.

Something very good will come from this...

Footnote

This was the last of the difficult days I would endure on this walk.

I Ain't That Kinda Guy

June 8, 2007

My apologies for no journal last night, but the three (okay, maybe six) of you might want to get used to it. We are staying at a place called the Homestead just outside of Ovando, Montana. It's an absolutely beautiful place, but communication is limited. I plan to update the journal every two or three days. The Homestead is by far the nicest place we have stayed.

With no phone, TV, or Internet, we read books in the evening and enjoy the Homestead's quiet peacefulness. They also have a nice rocking chair that I really like. It seems to be just what the doctor ordered for my back.

If I was the sort to admit to it, I would admit that my back has been a problem the entire journey. Once I get going, I am okay, but those first few steps in the morning and after I have been sitting for a while, are not a pretty sight. Perhaps I look (and feel) a bit old.

Yesterday was a very nice day on the road. The weather was excellent for walking with temperatures in the low 50s, clouds, and a light breeze. I guess it was Mother Nature's way of making up for the day before.

I am often asked if I think I will be in shape by the time I get to Kalispell. Well, I don't know, but if I am not, we will always think I should have been.

Something very good will come from this...

Cranky Dogs

June 9, 2007

Well, as it turns out, I have Internet access here at these nice folks' home office. This place is so quiet and peaceful. There are plenty of wild animals nearby, including a skunk (maybe related to Pepe Le Pew?) that were hanging around way too close for

191

me. I checked for skunks on the front porch before I walked out this morning.

Another very nice day here. I am walking down through a valley with lush, green rolling hills and tree-covered mountains on both sides.

Another dog issue today; three of them came running out from behind a building. I moved across the road to avoid them, but they followed me. I had the pepper spray out with the safety off and they were well within striking range when their owner came out and got them to back off. The owner didn't say anything to me, but he did give those dogs a piece of his mind.

Something very good will come from this...

Bowling and Golf Scores

June 10, 2007

More rain today. The good news is that it only rained for about half of the walk, so I did get some relief.

More folks stopped by to chat today. One lady came out from her house and walked down to meet me and walk back with me. We had a nice chat with lots of questions.

One guy stopped on the road and backed up to see if I was all right. I was afraid he was going to cause an accident.

I politely asked the road manager to write the journal today, but she told me that I don't want her to write it because she is still working on her "rebuttal." This is Montana now and most of the alleged incidents occurred in Utah and Idaho. Besides, most folk around here will take my side because I was born and raised here. Us Montana boys are pretty nice fellers.

I was also asked today if I am some sort of athlete. Well, allow me to tell you about my athletic prowess: my bowling and golf scores are often interchangeable (typically around 110).

Something very good will come from this...

Footnote

It turns out Bev never has written a rebuttal. Although she has never written anything, I can assure everyone that she has shared her thoughts with me verbally about some of my journal entries.

Old Horses

June 12, 2007

Another nice day today except for the wind. This part of Montana is very green this time of year. This makes the walking that much easier.

Yesterday, I spoke at a church in the sprawling metropolis of Helmville, Montana. I had a feeling I would be speaking somewhere nearby as several people had stopped to talk to us in the last few days. I think it went very well.

Tomorrow I will make the turn on to Highway 83, which will take me into the Flathead Valley. As the three/six of you know, I have not spent a lot of time thinking about how much further it is to Kalispell. It was simply too far for me to consider, but today, I did lift my head up long enough to get what I think was a whiff of the barn. If the wind is blowing the right way in the next week or so, that "old horse syndrome" might just kick in, and if it does, my advice for anyone in my way is to, well, please stand aside. Until then, I will keep the hat pulled down low and tight.

Something very good will come from this...

Whiff of the Barn

June 13, 2007

I have made it on to Highway 83. The weather today was very good with some rain toward the end. This walk up through the Swan Valley will be very scenic. I have been looking forward to this part of the walk since I left Gilbert in

February.

Today, for the first time, I walked past a road sign for Kalispell...Woohoo! Uh, let me repeat myself, WOO HOO!!!

I am now just less than 110 miles from Kalispell. I plan to take tomorrow off. That means that if the Good Lord is willin', and the creek don't rise, I will drop below the magical, almost mystical, dare I say mythical (yes, I dare) 100 mile mark on Friday.

First sign that I'm getting close.

Let's all hope the wind doesn't blow out of the north, because if I get another whiff of the barn, it could get ugly.

Something very good will come from this...

God's Country

June 15, 2007

Happy birthday, Cassandra! Not sure how old she is, but she is young enough to be my daughter, and as a matter of fact, she is.

I am now walking down through the Swan Valley. This is without a doubt the most scenic part of the journey. The road is lined with huge fir trees with many lakes and scenic mountains on both sides. Everything is very green right now.

I will be the first to admit that I don't make it to church every Sunday. Having said that, when you are out in the middle of beautiful country like this, I don't think you can get any closer to the Good Lord.

God's country indeed.

Someone asked Bev the other day if I was stubborn and she said yes. Perhaps I am a little teeny tiny bit stubborn, but I would submit a feller needs to be just a tad stubborn to walk this far.

I really do appreciate all the emails and words of encouragement.

Something very good will come from this...

Footnote
This walk down through the Swan Valley was sort of a victory lap for me. I enjoyed every day and looked forward to it.

No Chasing Butterflies

June 17, 2007

Things went well today; a few sprinkles, but overall, very nice. Norm and his wife Kim came out to visit with us. Norm and I went to high school together and graduated from Flathead High School in 1976. Norm walked with me and provided the entertainment.

The scenery is spectacular down through here, but the road is narrow, so I do have to watch where I am going; none of this wandering down the road chasing butterflies.

Something very good will come from this...

I Didn't Marry No Prairie Girl

June 18, 2007

Down through the Swan Valley I go. Mostly cloudy today with rain.

We had a nice lady by the name of Barb who stopped by to visit with us today. After we visited for a while, she took a picture of Bev and I, and one of the truck. She said that she wanted a picture to show her grandchildren when she told them about what happened to Kevin.

I need to let the three of you (or is it six now?) know that the road manager informed me in a very stern voice a few days back that she ain't no prairie girl. I will let the reader decide what that might have been about. I can only say that she had my undivided attention.

I read an editorial in the Daily Interlake that was published last Sunday. It was a great editorial that ended with the following:

> Adkins' daily online journal entries close with the prophetic statement: "something very good will come from this…"
> We think it already has.

Maybe it has, and maybe it hasn't. I have no way of knowing.

Something very good will come from this… and maybe many, many "something very goods."

Hug From a Stranger

June 19, 2007

More visitors today.

Often, as people pass by, I see their brake lights come on. They slow down and then keep going. This gentleman went by just as I left the truck to start my day on the road. I saw his brake lights go on and then he pulled over to the side of the road. He got out and started walking back toward me. When he got closer, it became obvious he was coming back to talk to me.

He walked right up and with out saying a word, he gave me a hug and started crying. He told me about his sons, one of which is in college and drinking heavily. He told me he worries that one day he could be in my shoes. He said that Kevin's Last Walk has helped him to continue to work with his son.

This chance meeting reminded me that while I have heard from many people, there are probably many more that Kevin's Last Walk has impacted how they handle their children. Even if just one kid gets an extra hug or an I Love You because of Kevin's Last Walk, it will be well worth it.

Today was much warmer with a high near 80 degrees. I am roughly 50 miles from Kalispell, which doesn't sound like much, unless, of course, you are walking.

As of this writing, the plan is to get to the bridge over the Flathead River by Saturday night. The reason being that I will cross it, oh, sometime around dark thirty Sunday morning when the traffic is very light (hopefully). The bridge is narrow and fairly long so, well, you get the drift. This route will allow me to cut about five miles off of the walk, and to be real honest (and I always am), I would probably swim that dag nab river to cut five miles off of the walk at this point.

Dang, I'm on a roll tonight. But as one of the three readers said to his mother when she commented that I was witty, "Don't give him too much credit. He has six hours to think up this stuff every day."

Something very good will come from this...

197

She's Always Right

June 21, 2007

I have made it to Swan Lake. The weather has been warm, but very nice. As long as it isn't snowing and blowing, I'm one happy camper.

I am pleased to report that my legs have returned from being MIA. They had no right to leave without checking with me, but at least they have returned. The road manager doesn't think they have returned. She thinks I just got a whiff of the barn. Hmm, well, it's conceivable that she could be right. Duh, what happily married man isn't married to a woman that is always right?

I guess this is where the wittiness ends. It's way past time for me to check my eyelids for pinholes.

Something very good will come from this...

Rarely Satisfied, but Always Happy

June 22, 2007

It looks like my eyelids are fine. I didn't find any pinholes. I will check again tonight.

Another warm day. Several people stopped to chat with me. It seems the media has done a great job of getting the word out.

Not much else to tell you about today, so here is one of my favorite quotes:

> "To laugh often and much to win the respect of intelligent people and affection of children; to earn the appreciation of honest critics and endure the betrayal of false friends; to appreciate beauty, to find the best in others; to leave the world a bit better, whether by a healthy child a garden patch or redeemed social condition; to know even one life has breathed easier because you have lived. This is to have succeeded."
> Ralph Waldo Emerson or Bessie Stanley
> (Depending on which website you trust.)

A toast to all who have made Kevin's Last Walk happen. You are a success. I guess the definition of success is in the eye of the beholder. Philosophically, I am rarely satisfied with what I do, but I am always happy.

Something very good will come from this...

Need to Contact My Legal Staff

June 23, 2007

Short day today. I met an 89-year-old man walking along on the trail I found that got me off the highway for a few miles. He was a photographer during World War II. He still gets around quite well. I thanked him for his service to our country.

Apparently, I may not have carefully thought through a few comments I made about an uncle of mine on May 23rd. It has been pointed out that I only have one surviving uncle, which means that a person skilled in the art of deductive reasoning (which apparently he is) could figure out who I was referring to. I have been asked to retract my remarks regarding his ability to "tell stories." Well, uh, maybe I'm not prepared to retract those remarks just yet. I will be forwarding these remarks to my legal staff. I have also asked for any documentation that might be available to shed more light on this "situation." The problem here is that none of us have particularly good memories and as time goes on, well, you get the drift.

Something very good will come from this...

You Can Use My Baby Wipes

June 25, 2007

Yesterday I finished just outside of Kalispell. Some old friends from Missouri drove out to spend the day with us. Bev says that Cindy is already certified as a road manager. I don't think my friend Bill graduated from road manager school quite as fast.

One of the things that I worried about on this walk was the possibility that I might need to take a walk into the woods with some toilet paper or baby wipes. I kept a handful of baby wipes in my backpack the entire 1,400 miles, and as it turns out, I never used them. That's right, 1,400 miles and no "number two" in the woods. On this day, however, a certain someone that came out to walk with me needed them for a "walk in the woods." I gave him the bag of baby wipes and told him I didn't want the bag back.

I am now getting very close to tying a bow in this. Time for everyone to start asking how it feels, what are you going to do now, are you going to continue speaking, do you think "something very good" has come from this, etc. Well, I don't think I have had time to digest all of this. I have been on the inside looking out. The view for me has been very different from others. I have been focused on getting my miles in everyday, getting to every speaking engagement, and doing my best not to get run over.

As far as I am concerned, this has been one incredible, successful journey. How it will be seen by other folks is, well, up to them to decide. This journey has given a number of people—including me—the chance to get involved and make a difference in a way they probably didn't know they could, which I consider to be "something very good."

Okay, I have had time to digest a smidge more. Yup, it feels very, very, fantabulous to be here. I am sure that Sunday will not be the last time I tell the story about what happened to Kevin. As for "something very good," well, stay tuned.

On a more serious note, there was fresh snow on the mountains here today. It's hard to believe that I did not have one "weather day" this entire journey. As I keep saying, "I would rather be lucky than good."

I am scheduled to speak seven times this week, so I will be busy.

Can anyone tell I need to get some sleep?

Something very good will come from this...

Not Too Deeply Troubled

June 28, 2007

Well, it's official, I have arrived in Kalispell! Today my daughter, Cassandra, walked the last five miles with me to the staging area for the finish on Sunday. We actually stopped in the parking lot of Lowe's, strategically situated next to the Starbucks. We will walk three miles on Sunday to Majestic Valley Arena, which is three miles north of Kalispell. That's right, an extra three miles, which *should* be a piece of cake.

Did I mention that I have arrived in Kalispell?

In the last three days, I have spoken six different times, which is plenty for me. I started doing some math and figured out that I have spoken at least 27 times just in Idaho and Montana alone. It's kind of hard to believe when I stand back and look at it.

Did I mention I have arrived in Kalispell?

Maybe I should put it a different way: If any one of the three of you know anyone who bet against me, well, you might want to let them know they need to prepare to cover their bet. I think I should make it just a tad clearer: I HAVE ARRIVED IN KALISPELL!

Trinity, Collin, and Cassandra have also arrived and I guess you all know what that means: the road manager is very tired. There is something about chasing after grandkids that wears her out.

Dang, not sure if I mentioned something you might find interesting: I have officially arrived in Kalispell!

On another subject, my one and only uncle still claims to be troubled by my remarks, but maybe only some of the time. He didn't seem to be too deeply troubled while he was working over a piece of cake and two different flavors of ice cream last night.

Three more things I need to mention before I finish. I have arrived, I am here, and I am, uh, well, in Kalispell!

Something very good will come from this...

201

Ordinary Man, Extraordinary Journey

July 1, 2007

Well, I guess it's official. I have completed this 1,400 mile journey!

Today, along with about 200 other folks, I made the final three and a half mile journey to Majestic Valley Arena and most importantly, we all made it safely. Many people worked hard to make this happen, including several members of the Montana Highway Patrol and the Flathead County Sheriff's office. They did a great job of getting us all there safely and I am very thankful.

I have been asked several times what it feels like to finish such a journey. Well, I am not sure it has hit me just yet, so stay tuned.

There wasn't a single sick day or bad weather day. I won't say that the weather always cooperated (because it didn't), but when I needed it most, the wind was at my back.

Bev says that I scared her several times during this journey, and I guess I have to admit, I scared me sometimes.

Okay, I have let it sink in a bit more. I find it difficult to believe that I walked from Arizona to Montana. I am glad I didn't know how difficult it would be. The countless hours spent icing sore hips, knees, and feet. The army of people that made sure we had a place to sleep and that I was where I needed to be when I needed to be there.

I have said it before and I will say it again: I am just the dude who did the walking and the talking.

Successfully completing Kevin's Last Walk was part of the Good Lord's plan for me. There is no way that I could have completed this journey without His help. I am sure that the Good Lord and Kevin were watching over me the entire journey. It wasn't perfect. I battled fatigue, pain, traffic, roads, dogs, and weather all the way.

The "finish" for most was a celebration of my accomplishment. Friends and family came in from as far away as Alaska and

Pennsylvania. They came by bus, car, and plane. We had big gatherings, small gatherings and, of course, met a few friends for coffee, hugs, smiles, and tears.

For me, it's bittersweet. Yes, finishing Kevin's Last Walk is a major accomplishment, but it also means that it's time to say a final "goodbye" to Kevin. Like everyone else, I had been looking forward (at least physically) to this day. I do not look forward to laying Kevin to rest.

I guess in a way, Kevin's Last Walk was an excuse for me to spend a little more time with my son and that time is coming to an end. I know that everyone reading this book is rooting for me to find "closure" by completing this journey. I don't honestly know what closure means, but if it means that everything is suddenly okay, it's not. I would venture to guess that when it comes to losing a child, there is no such thing as closure, there is only an easing of the pain, which this journey did do for me.

I give thanks to those that made this happen. First and foremost, I give thanks to the Good Lord. Clearly it was in His plans to allow me to finish this journey safely and successfully! Next, of course is my wife, Bev. Without her love and support, this journey would not have happened. The death of a child often causes the breakup of marriages. For us, it has brought us closer. All of the credit goes to the Good Lord and her; it's as simple as that.

Something very good will come from this...

Chapter 23

Laying Kevin to Rest

The day after the official finish of Kevin's Last Walk, we had a small private ceremony to lay Kevin to rest on our land near Ashley Lake.

A friend of mine created a head stone out of metal. My uncle and neighbors cleared an area at the back of our land and made a corral (for lack of a better term). We chose the site on our land where there is a beautiful view of the valley below.

In the days leading up to the finish, I thought a lot about how I wanted to lay Kevin to rest. I offered the opportunity to several people to lead some sort of prayer service. They all politely declined. At the time, I wondered why they didn't want to. I am not good at quoting chapter and verse out of the Bible and, the truth be told, I was close to tired of talking. I guess this was a message from the Good Lord that this service had to come from me. I decided on doing something short and simple. Imagine that.

We all gathered around Kevin's ashes in a circle and joined hands. I started by reading the following poem that I had written on a particularly beautiful day during the walk in northern Idaho.

Your Place

I know this is your place
I will get you there
To that wide open space
Where the eagles watch

205

And the air so fresh
This is your place
You always wanted to be
Where tall are the trees
And the grass so green
The mountains of wonder
Covered in white
Where you can watch over it all
And finally you find peace

I then asked everyone to finish the following sentence: "I am thankful for..."

Next, we went to a nearby lake for an old-fashioned picnic. The children went fishing, swimming, and threw rocks in the water, while the adults relaxed in the shade or played horseshoes.

As for me, well, I relaxed in the shade and sipped on lemonade and an occasional cup of coffee. As I sat there in the cool shade of huge pine trees overlooking Bitterroot Lake, I thought about all that had happened since Kevin passed away.

Those most painful days, nights, weeks, and months after Kevin died.

Standing in the kitchen when the idea to walk to Montana came to me.

Those kids in Payson, Arizona that did a penny drive for me.

That hill before Flagstaff Arizona when I wondered if I had bit off more than I could chew.

Friends and family who were so very supportive, but probably worried that I wouldn't be able to make it.

The guy near Fountain Hills, Arizona that saluted me and gave me a flag.

The Flagstaff police officer who stopped to thank me for speaking at his son's school a week north of Flagstaff.

The guy who stopped to talk to me near Page, Arizona and then handed me $5 and told me to get something to eat with it.

The trucker and the couple driving an RV who both stopped in the middle of the road in Montana to offer words of encouragement.

The lady in Idaho Falls who, while standing outside of a restaurant after dinner, said they would never forget me, but doubted that I would remember them.

The parents and children alike who listened to me speak, read an article about Kevin, or saw it on TV, and then went home and gave a loved one a hug, or maybe held them a little closer for a little longer.

The army of people who made Kevin's Last Walk happen. Teachers, principals, social workers, friends, family, notMYkid, Todd Stottlemyre, and of course, my blushing bride. They all stepped out of their comfort zone to contribute.

I wondered if Bev kept track of how many times I asked her, "How much further to the top?"

The guy that I had never met, who pulled off to the side of the road, walked up to me, gave me a hug, and started crying.

The note I found in my backpack when I finished the walk that read,

> "Oh, Lord," I cried. "My heart will break. Nothing can ever stop this ache. Oh! Lord, My son is gone."
>
> "Gone?" God said. "No, your son is not gone,

because as long as you have memories in your heart, he lives on. My child, don't you know I care, I won't give you more than you can bear. Life and Death are my choice. Trust my wisdom and rejoice. Wipe away the tear from your eye, for there's no longer need to cry. My Son died so you could have eternal life, now he's with me, in Paradise. I watch all my children from Heaven above. When harvest time comes, I take them home in love. I alone am God. I know what's best. Trust me and I will give your heart rest. I am the King, for each life I have a plan. I hold your future in the palm of my hand. I'm the Good Shepherd and I know my own. You are never forsaken or left alone. I know you loved him, but I love him more. I held his hand and gently led him through the door. He's more alive now than he was before. He's happier now than he's ever been. In this perfect world without hurt or sin. Asleep? No! We walked together today, and he watched you as you knelt to pray. He smiled and said, 'They miss me you know. Do they understand why I had to go? I loved them and I know they loved me. Tell them I'm happy, tell them I'm free. It's wonderful here, don't weep for me. We'll soon be together for eternity."

God never makes mistakes. His hand is on us all. He alone decides when and who to call. Apart for only a while, he's gone one step before, so he can stand beside Jesus and meet you at Heaven's door.

I don't remember who, when, or how this note got in my backpack.

I thought about Kevin. With roles of father and son clearly reversed, I hoped he was looking down and smiling. Kevin, I hope you approve.

Chapter 24

Conclusion

I've come to accept what happened and realize that I can't change it. I should clarify this by saying that I accept it with the deepest sorrow. This is certainly not how I had my life scripted. My plan for all of my children was to grow up, get a great job, get married, and start cranking out grandchildren. When I got to the rocking chair age, they would take turns changing my urine bags. We all would live happily ever after and, most importantly, I would die before they did. But as the saying goes, "If you wanna hear God laugh, tell Him your plans."

It's been difficult for me to accept the fact that God causes or allows everything, but I have. Most Christians will tell you that they understand this, but probably haven't really come to grips with the "everything" part of it. When you really come to grips with it, it sets you free. God has a plan for all of us, a plan we know nothing about, and we have to trust Him.

I have been told many times that Kevin's Last Walk was an extraordinary journey and an amazing tribute to Kevin.

I think it's the least I could do.

I have also heard that "something very good" has come from this, and I know that it has, but for me, I don't know if it's the "something very good" that Kevin told me about.

Perhaps I will never know what the "something very good" is, and perhaps that is precisely the point; I should spend the rest of my life making "something very good" come from Kevin's death.

Some of you are probably wondering, well, what are you going to do next? All I can say is, stay tuned! For many more stories and pictures, visit www.kevinslastwalk. com.

By the way, what is your "something very good?"

May God bless you and keep your children safe.

Something very good will come from this...